CURSE BE GONE

Reversal and Protection Magick to Break Hexes, Defend Yourself, Banish Negative Influences & More

SOFIA VISCONTI

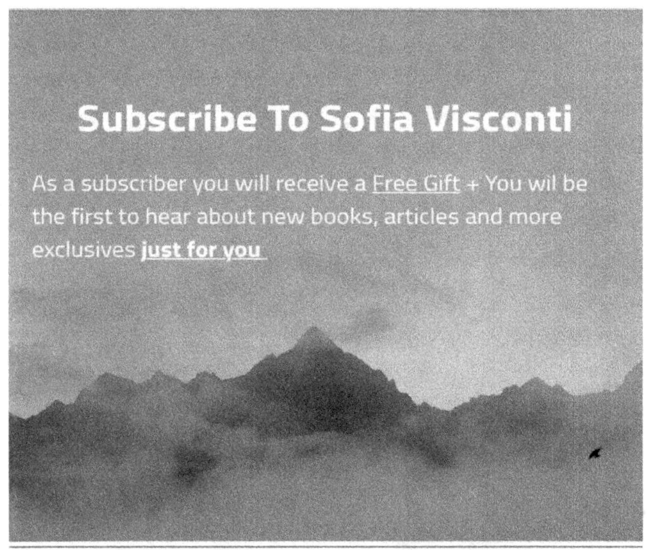

Subscribe To Sofia Visconti

As a subscriber you will receive a Free Gift + You wil be the first to hear about new books, articles and more exclusives just for you

CLICK HERE

CONTENTS

INTRODUCTION

A witch ought never to be frightened in the darkest forest because she should be sure in her soul that the most terrifying thing in the forest was her. – Terry Pratchett

Us witches know that magick is real and that it is powerful. Sure, we can't launch fireballs out of our hands or rustle up a big win on the lottery—after all, it's magick not miracles—but we know, deep in the place within our guts where our intuition lies, that magick can achieve many things that others wouldn't dare think possible. Whether it's bringing greater prosperity into your life or helping you find that special someone, magick can be used for all sorts of purposes to great effect.

Note the use of the alternative spelling "magick" here. This is to distinguish the practices of true witchcraft and sorcery from the sort of stage magic a magician may perform at a child's party (Kraig, 2010). We're not pulling rabbits out of a hat, here; we are making material change in the universe based on our intentions, actions, and energies.

Perhaps, you are already familiar with magick. In that case, the book in your hands will act as an excellent supplement to your preexisting magickal library, helping you to add to your current repertoire. But you may, instead, be someone who is only just starting out, interested in magick but unsure what it's about or where to begin. It makes sense, then, to add a brief introduction to the practices of magick and witchcraft before I continue with why magickal self-defense is important. Indeed, many advanced witches agree that defensive magick is the best place for newbie witches to start, so you've come to the right place.

What Is Magick?

Magick, like religion, has likely existed since time immemorial. While religion focuses on the actions of deities and other cosmic beings—often petitioning them for aid or trying to ascend to be closer to them—magick instead draws attention to the self and what we can do using our own power. The two are often intertwined to create a cohesive system of belief that involves both worship and spell-craft. This can be seen throughout history, such as with the Ancient Greeks, as well as in the modern day, in neopagan religions such as Wicca and Druidism (Fowler, 1995).

Indeed, so common is this intermingling of magick and religion into Wicca in particular that many believe all witches are Wiccan. This, however, is not the case. One can follow any religion—even Christianity—or none at all and still be a witch because of the already-stated distinction between the two spiritual systems. So, while pretty much all Wiccans are witches, not all witches are Wiccan.

To better understand magick, it makes sense to come to a common definition. There is an often repeated quote from infamous occultist Aleister Crowley—who was not without his problems—that states that magick is the "Science and Art that provokes Change in conformity with the Will" (*What is magic? Aleister Crowley explains*, 2020). The actual practice of magick involves more than intention, however.

Magick presupposes the existence of typically unseen forces and energies that can still, with practice, be perceived and manipulated. These energies run through all things, from the universe as a whole down to a grain of sand. We each contain within us part of the divine spark of creation, showing the symbiotic way we exist with the world and creatures that surround us. We all also have an energy that is specific to the type of being we are, as well as who we are as individuals, too. This means that while each lavender plant is an individual, it will still carry the same sort of traits that other plants like it do—something that we'll see when we come to correspondences in Chapter 3.

The universe itself is alive with all these forces, working to its own rhythm, but with practice, we can tap into this and manipulate the flows of energy to do our bidding. The notion that everything contains some form of energy or consciousness—no matter how different that looks from our own—is called "animism." While this might take a while to get your head around if you've been raised in a Christian culture, it is actually a common belief in non-Western spiritualities and religions.

Additionally, the belief in the divinity of the universe itself is "pantheism." Many witches recognize divinity and the universe to be one and the same thing, although some perceive the divine to extend beyond even this, existing outside the boundaries of space and time. This belief system is called "panentheism." Those are a lot of words that might take a while to get used to, but knowing the basics of these different belief systems allows you to come to your own conclusion about spiritual matters and how these then go on to intersect with the practice of witchcraft and magick. This is important because it is by reaching out with our own energy and interacting with those of others that we achieve our magickal aims. They can be collaborated with and manipulated in such a way that the change reverberates throughout the cosmos, causing our desired effect.

As a simple example, we may pour our intentions into a bay leaf with a wish written on it, and then burn it over a candle to release that intention and energy into the world. Before we know it, we've passed the test we needed to take, have secured a new job, or landed ourselves a hot date at the weekend. All of this is possible with magick and more.

Debunking Myths About Magick

Unfortunately, there are a number of myths and misconceptions out there about magick and witchcraft which are unhelpful to hold when learning more about these sacred practices. I've already debunked two of these: the idea that magick doesn't really exist and that all witches are Wiccan. As I have shown, both of these beliefs are false, borne out of ignorance of the occult— understandable, really, when you consider that the word "occult" can be defined as "hidden from view" and "not easily apprehended or understood (Merriam-Webster, n.d.-a). Most of us carry at least one or two misconceptions about this because we simply do not know any better. It's just how we were brought up in a culture that sees the occult as mere superstition or something to be mocked.

To help dismantle these ideas which blinker us from the realities of magick, I'll now list a few more of these myths and debunk them so that you have a clear understanding of what is and is not true. This is vital because believing any of these falsities will only be a hindrance to learning what is to come. It's important, then, to get a grip on these basics before you continue on your path.

Magick Is Evil

There is often talk about "white magick" and "black magick," and many people think that only the latter exists. In this dualistic framework, white magick is seen as that which is beneficial—encouraging healing, bringing prosperity, increasing the chances of finding love, and so on. Black magick, on the other hand, is that which is baneful, such as cursing enemies, forcing someone to fall in love with someone else, or binding people's actions and free will.

However, instead of me saying that black magick is not "real magick," or that it is forbidden, I am going to follow a different track by saying this: Magick is a tool. Just like a knife can be used for cutting veggies or stabbing someone, magick can be used for nice or nasty purposes. In this respect, then, it is *amoral*, meaning it lacks a moral component whatsoever. It is, instead, the will of the practitioner that can be said to be good or bad.

There is also the quandary of what is good or bad, in the first place. Let's take a look at two examples: Firstly, if someone were to cast a spell for them to get a job, but it then prevented someone who was living in poverty from gaining employment, can that not be said to be harmful magic? Secondly, if a witch binds a bully who then cannot abuse whoever it is they are picking on, can that not be said to be beneficial magic? Morality isn't as simple as the dualism between black and white tells us. Instead, there is a continuum that is every shade of gray imaginable. This is the real reason why saying "magick is evil" or "all magick is black magick" is unhelpful.

Moreover, there are other issues with this characterization of magick as "white = good, black = evil." In popular culture, black magick is usually associated with African diasporic religions such as Hoodoo and Haitian Vodou, both of which are often mistakenly called "voodoo" (Murphy, 1990; Newman, 2023). On the other hand, depictions of white witches practicing "good" magick in films and television shows such as *Sabrina the Teenage Witch, Buffy the Vampire Slayer*, and others, all depict the kind caster as a white person—usually a pretty young woman but sometimes a maternal older lady. This shows that it is usually the magick practitioner that is considered "Other," in turn causing the magick itself to be racialized, demonized as "black magick," and therefore thought of as evil. We should, then, be considerate of the thorny issue of implicit racial bias when using these terms. Often, it is better to be specific about what you mean rather than reverting to the black/white dichotomy, such as by saying "baneful magick" to refer to that which aims to harm.

Only Women Can Be Witches
A witch is simply someone of any gender who practices witchcraft, even if pop culture often depicts only women, as I covered above. There is a belief that it was only women, too, who were burned at the stake

during the witch hunts. In fact, around 10–15% of people who were burned—or hanged, as was more often the case—after being accused of witchcraft were male (*Witchcraft: Eight myths and misconceptions,* n.d.). This means that we should not gatekeep the term from people who identify with it because we all have a collective history tied to the persecution of individuals, usually living on the margins of society, as witches.

Sometimes, this belief comes from the erroneous claim that (cisgender) women are more magickally inclined than those assigned male at birth. Frankly, this is hogwash: There is nothing about a uterus or other reproductive organs that provide someone with more magickal ability than those without them. This is simply gatekeeping the terminology from people based on prejudice against them. While the intent to lift up women comes from a good place, doing so in this way is spreading misinformation and becomes exclusionary of anyone not in the "in-group." We should avoid these myths at all costs and instead work towards a witchcraft that is inclusive of all who are interested in it.

You Have to Be Initiated or Born Into Being a Witch

Some people are fortunate enough to be born to a family of witches. Some people, too, seek out traditions that require initiation in order to join them, such as Gardnerian Wicca. However, just because this is sometimes the case doesn't mean it always is.

While it may give you a head start in training to be a witch if one or both of your parents are also witches—particularly because folk magick traditions contain a lot of oral history that is passed down through the generations—it is not essential to have "witch blood," as some call it. Being born into a family of witches does not make your magick naturally stronger than those who have come to find the practice themselves. It just means you're more likely to have learned about it at a younger age.

As well as this, back in 1989, Scott Cunningham published his famous *Wicca: A Guide for the Solitary Practitioner*, which put forward a form of Wicca that could be practiced by the individual without initiation into a coven. While some people do go on to choose to make their own self-initiation ritual if they are a solitary practitioner, this is not required, either. To be a witch, one must simply practice witchcraft, and there are plenty of practices outside of Wicca, such as Traditional Witchcraft, which require no formal initiation into the craft unless the witch decides to create one for themselves.

However, it should be said that some practices are closed. This means that certain traditions shut out outsiders, usually because colonialism put these practices at risk of appropriation, theft, or forced assimilation into the dominant culture. For instance, Native American spirituality is closed to those who are not Indigenous, and some practices may even be closed to those not within a certain tribe. This is because this spirituality came under threat during colonialism, and certain practices were stolen and bastardized while the people they originated from were punished for carrying out their own religious beliefs. In order to protect the rich heritage and legacy of Indigenous cultures, these practices have essentially had their doors closed to strangers and can only be shared in special circumstances when the tribe in question gives an invitation to outsiders. It is important to honor this desire for privacy and respect, and that means not cherrypicking from these practices. Other closed practices include Hoodoo, Haitian Vodou, and Kabbalah.

This idea of practices being closed differs from malicious gatekeeping because it is an effort to protect marginalized cultures from theft and appropriation, as well as acknowledging that certain practices require certain knowledge that could only be obtained from living within a specific culture your whole life. However, there are fortunately plenty of open practices from across the world that can be engaged with to create your own spiritual system, such as Wicca, Traditional Witchcraft, and various European folk magicks and ancient religions. It is for this reason that it is unnecessary to cause upset by delving into practices closed to you.

You Have to Be Psychic to Be a Witch
While it certainly helps to be in touch with

psychism if one is to practice witchcraft, this is by no means essential. However, it should be said that, as Mat Auryn (2020a) states in his book *Psychic Witch*, everyone has latent psychic powers. We are conditioned out of having these, typically at some point in childhood, because of societal norms and denials of the magick that surrounds us. How many children come across as spooky, talking to things that other people can't see or having imaginary friends who seem a little bit too real? While, of course, not all instances of this are because children are communicating with spirits—indeed, most will be the product of children's wonderfully overactive imaginations—there are occasionally times when the behavior of a child can only be explained as supernatural. Unfortunately, though, we train our children to ignore these experiences, and over time, they are shut off from their "clair senses." The psychic senses that are shut off from most of us are as follows (Auryn, 2020a):

- **Clairvoyance:** The ability to see things that others can't, such as spirits.
- **Clairaudience:** The ability to hear things that others can't.
- **Clairgustance:** The same as above, except for taste.
- **Clairtangency:** The same as above, except for touch and physical sensations upon the body.
- **Clairalience:** The same as above, except for smell.

- **Clairempathy:** The ability to detect and feel the emotions of others.
- **Clairsentience:** The feeling of physical sensations within the body without a mundane explanation.
- **Claircognizance:** Knowing information that you could not otherwise know.

These latent powers can be trained and tapped into with some effort.

Additionally, anyone can learn to use tools to practice divination, which is the uncovering of secret information and delving into what the future may hold should all things stay on the same trajectory—for we cannot deny the uncanny ability of free will to throw a spanner in the works! There are plenty of books on the market to help you pick up the basics of Tarot cards, for instance—indeed, I even wrote one myself (Visconti, 2019).

A word of caution, however: Usually, the hearing or seeing of things that others cannot perceive can have mundane explanations. Carbon monoxide poisoning, for example, does very strange things to the brain. On top of this, estimates place the incidence rate of psychosis in the American population anywhere between 1.5% and 5%(Calabrese and Al Kahlili, 2023). Psychosis is the existence of hallucinations and delusions—unusual thought patterns that are fervently believed—usually together but not always. This means that any new experiences that seem unexplainable should, first of all, be investigated for mundane causes such as these illnesses and others.

To be responsible witches, we must distinguish between the magickal and the mundane often, as otherwise, we can easily fall down rabbit holes that result in very tricky mental situations. While psychism and magick are both very much real, we should still be skeptical to a degree and practice discernment before jumping to the conclusion that something is an otherworldly or spiritual occurrence. Distinguishing between natural and magickal causes is covered further in Chapter 2.

The Importance of Magickal Self-Defense

Magick can be used for many a good thing. However, it's not always so rosy. Some magickal practitioners will have no qualms in directing the universe to wreak havoc against others, such as their rivals or those that they feel have "wronged" them in some way—whether or not this is actually the case is all rather academic when you have a curse hurtling towards you.

Sometimes, too, our magick acts like a magnet, drawing the attention of entities we'd rather not tangle with. In his book Psychic Witch, Mat Auryn (2020a) talks about being pestered by spirits constantly, only to realize he is the only witch within his area, and so, the magick he is practicing is drawing the attention of inquisitive spirits to his home like moths to a flame. While most of these spirits are harmless and simply curious about what's going on, you may not want them there at all, or you may, in rare instances, attract the attention of one whom no one would want around. Spirits are like people, after all, and while most are happy to go about their own lives, some like to be bothersome.

It is for these reasons that many of us suggest beginner witches start their practice by learning protection magick, as I said above. To this, we can also add reversals and banishings as it is better to be able to do something before an issue potentially springs up on you, perhaps catching you unawares.

Don't fear, though: While it is always best to keep yourself protected in a variety of ways at all times, it is unlikely that you will come under any of these attacks. However, because they can cause many deleterious effects if they are made, it is good to make sure your shields are up to protect you in the event of them happening. Better to be safe than sorry, as the old saying goes, and we witches know the powers contained in such old adages.

This book, then, is a one-stop source for creating your own psychic and magickal arsenal and warding against harm created by irresponsible practitioners or spirits with a malevolent (or simply annoying) agenda.

Having been a practicing witch myself for many years now—indeed, I've authored a lot of books on the matter—I am in the position to pass on the wisdom that I have learned during my own magickal journey. This book represents the best of my knowledge about self-defensive magick. Read on, and become prepared for anything to come your way.

CHAPTER 1
UNDERSTANDING MAGICK FOR SELF-DEFENSE

Great results can be achieved with small forces. – Sun Tzu

It is wise to first gain an understanding of what magickal self-defense looks like before trying to dive headfirst into spells. Having a sound knowledge of the practices of magickal self-defenses—including where they come from and their historical manifestations—will allow you to plot out what your own arsenal needs to include.

It is also important to talk about our responsibilities as magickal practitioners and our codes of ethics. As I have already said, magick itself is a tool—an amoral apparatus that you control to enact your will. Ethics applies to these intentions as well as the wider ramifications of a spell's outcome. It is good practice to think about these ethical considerations before practicing magic, and so, I will deal with them in this chapter, too.

The Basics of Self-Defensive Magick

There are a number of different types of spells that make up self-defensive magick. Some are proactive, meaning you do them to prevent harm coming your way or to catch it before it penetrates into you. Others are reactive steps you would take should you come under psychic or magickal attack. In this latter category, these can be broken down further into the reversal of hexes—which sometimes also includes a return-to-sender spell—and the banishing of negative energies and malevolent spirits.

Protective Magick

Spells for protection, sometimes called "apotropaic magick" in more academic texts, are frequently referred to as "wards." Looking at the definition for this word, Merriam-Webster (n.d.-c) describes a ward as "the action or process of guarding." This is an appropriate definition for this type of magick, too. Wards are essentially a way of guarding yourself and what's yours from outside interference. They are the metaphorical lock on your door that keeps out the things you don't want coming in.

Many practitioners talk about "layered" wards. This means having multiple wards at once aimed at different things and protecting you in different ways. For example, many witches ward themselves personally from negative influence using an amulet that they wear on their person. They may then hang an iron horseshoe above their front door to prevent evil from entering the house—as well as to encourage luck, for spells can be about more than one thing at once—as is an old folk charm from England (King, 2016). Finally, they may also craft a "witch bottle," originally designed to protect against witchcraft but now commonly used as an aggressive means of protection which "bites back" against any untoward influences attempting to make their way into a property (Meier, 2019). We will cover witch bottles more below, but suffice to say, these examples show the many ways different wards can be used for the protection of both persons and property at the same time.

Additionally, the more wards you have, the harder it is for negativity or harm to break through. It's like locks, again: Only one on the door means that, with force, someone or something may be able to break through, but several layered up makes it a much more formidable target.

Reversal Magick: Hex-Breaking and Return-to-Sender

Reversal magick is reactive. This means you carry it out when you sense or divine that you have been affected by a hex, curse, or psychic attack. I'll cover the differences between these in the next chapter, as well as how to figure out whether or not you are under the effect of these.

There are two ways that you may go about doing a reversal: You may choose to break the spell to release its influence on you. The alternative is to go harder and perform a return-to-sender. This essentially takes the curse and reverts it back to whence it came.

There is much debate over the ethics of this in the witchcraft community as it can be seen as a form of baneful magic, in the same way that the aggressive witch bottle above may also be seen—due to the fact it attacks that which tries to enter. It is up to you to decide, given the circumstances, whether or not you will simply dismantle an attack against you or return it to whoever sent it. However, it is worth knowing more about both of these methods, and so, each will be covered in depth in Chapter 6.

Banishing

Sometimes, entities you don't want in your space will come in, usually to be nosey and see what's going on. Magick can, but won't always, draw the attention of curious spirits as I detailed in the previous chapter. If you'd rather have no truck with them, you can politely but firmly tell them to leave. Most will do so. A thorough cleanse of your space after this—we'll get to what cleansing is in Chapter 4—is enough to revert the energy of your home back to normal.

However, there are rarer circumstances in which

more persistent visitors, who may or may not be causing trouble, come to your space. In these instances, you need to be a bit more heavy-handed. A banishing is in order when you cannot get an entity to leave your space with polite words and a nudge out the door with a cleanse followed by a more stern command to go. A banishing is essentially a spell performed to kick them out of the space, and it is often then followed up by renewing wards or creating new ones to prevent them from coming back.

Even if you have zero interest in spirit work, it is best to only banish when absolutely necessary. You wouldn't throw rocks at the salesperson on your doorstep: Telling them you're not interested is enough to get rid of them. But when things start to go awry and the interfering being won't leave, it is appropriate to bring out the big guns, as it were.

While it is rare indeed to need to banish an entity, it does unfortunately happen sometimes. That's why it's best to be prepared with knowledge in advance so that you're not scrambling around trying to create a ritual when one is sorely needed. Knowledge and planning is a key part of being a witch, and so, in Chapter 6, I'll go through the basics of banishing.

The History and Cultural Significance of Self-Defensive Magick

Self-defensive spells and charms have been around as long as magick has—a very long time, indeed. To get a better idea of what this can involve, it's worth having a look at history to see how people have protected themselves over the millennia. I'll start where it makes the most sense, with the Ancient World, before looking at Medieval magick, too. Finally, we'll take a look at examples of some of the most common forms of self-defensive magick, as well as at the concept of the evil eye, which is commonly spoken about in the folk magick traditions of Europe and pops up on social media as a trending topic periodically.

The Ancient World

The cultures of antiquity are not a monolith. They do have protective magick in common in the vaguest sense, but the symbolism and methods used vary. I'll outline just a few examples below so that you have a wider knowledge base than if I delved more deeply into just one area. This will allow you to compare and contrast the types of magick being used, which will help you when it comes to crafting your own spells.

The Ancient Greeks

The Ancient Greeks had many different forms of protective symbols. One of these was the decapitated head of Medusa—the gorgon slain by Perseus— whose head, in mythology, was placed upon Athena's shield, the Aegis. Another symbol was the disembodied eye, which harkens to the use of the famous blue nazar— sometimes known as a "mati"—which is used for protection against the evil eye (covered more below) in the present day (Habib, 2017; Hargitai, 2018; Volandes,

2020).

A form of reactive magick can be seen in their so-called "curse tablets," known as *defixiones* in Latin and *katadesmoi* in Ancient Greek. These were essentially spells that bound the actions of an enemy. While these tablets were commonly used to silence or incapacitate rivals, or to tie a desired lover to one's self, some are classed as spells of justice. These were typically encouragements for thieves to return stolen objects by punishing them in the meantime, usually through the petitioning of a deity to dole out penalties on the magickal practitioner's behalf. Magick practitioners put much effort into showing the deity in question the righteousness of their cause and how their actions were proportionate to the harm done to them. These tablets were made by carving a pliable material (usually lead), rolling it up, and piercing it with a nail. There is the potential, however, that other materials were used and they have been lost to time due to decay, such as papyrus. The rolled-up tablet was then placed within an appropriately magickal place, such as a grave or a temple to the god petitioned (Versnel, 1991).

The Romans

The Romans had a curiously popular amulet called a "fascinum." This was, essentially, an oversized erect phallus, sometimes with wings, typically worn around the neck—very obscene, indeed! However, it was thought that this very obscenity, along with the idea of the phallus being a sign of potency, would ward against evil and ill health. It was considered so powerful and so widely used that such amulets were even given to children by worried parents (Angel, 2013; Lóránt, 2016).

On top of this, the curse tablets named above by the Ancient Greeks continued to be popular following the colonization of Greece by the Roman empire (Blakemore, 2016).

The Ancient Egyptians

The Ancient Egyptians had many different magickal symbols, just like the other cultures explored here. One item they used was akin to a magick wand formed out of hippopotamus ivory, which was used in childbirth magick as well as buried with the deceased for their protection in the afterlife (Larson, 2019). It was frequently carved with protective emblems associated with their gods, such as cats, frogs, lions, and serpents (Vink, 2016).

An interesting part of Ancient Egyptian magick is the role of sound. When completing a magickal ritual, one had to speak the correct words in the correct way, including the secret names of the deities called upon. It was also thought that causing a ruckus could drive away evil spirits—something that many witches do today, as well, calling it "sound cleansing," as I will explain in Chapters 4 and 6 (Pinch, 2011).

One type of popular amulet was made from papyrus (Dieleman, 2015). On this, a spell would be written out, and it would be rolled up and worn on a string around the neck—much more modest than the Roman fascinum!

Ancient West Asia and North Africa

In the empires of west Asia and north Africa (WANA), serpents were a potent symbol of protection, as indeed they were elsewhere in places like Greece, likely because of the cultural exchanges that these societies had. In Greece, the household spirit Agathos Daimon was often depicted as a snake and was thought to protect the people within the home. The WANA region went further than Greece, however, as it was deities within this area that featured characteristics of snakes. In particular, they, too, were typically seen as protectors of places rather than objects or people (Clark, n.d.; Golding, 2013).

Various ancient cultures of the WANA region also used "incantation bowls," sometimes called "demon bowls." These were basins decorated with a magickal inscription around the inside and buried upside down on the thresholds of the property. These were thought to trap evil spirits before they could enter (Murphy and Susalla, 2016).

Medieval Times

Despite the Christian culture that predominated by the time of the Medieval period, folk magick was still popular; indeed, it never died out, it just became syncretic with Christianity and its cosmology. This meant that pagan aspects were absorbed into Christianity in a complex way that involved both the keeping of some aspects of the old culture and the adaptation of others to fit the new worldview. We can see that this has happened with many other religions throughout history: The Romans did it with many of the cultures of the places they conquered, and enslaved Africans merged their own cultures with the Christianity taught to them on plantations to keep the magick alive, albeit in a slightly altered way.

During medieval times, however, there was a delineation between witches—who were thought to be casters of malefic magic—and the cunning folk, who were considered to be helpful and even thwarters of witchcraft (Baker, 2014). There were many charms and spells used to protect against a variety of different threats. I'll cover a few below to give an idea of the most prominent forms of protection during this time.

Witch Bottles

I have already mentioned witch bottles above, but it is worth discussing them in more detail because, in many ways, they are the precursor to the now very popular use of jar spells in modern witchcraft. A witch's bottle was a glass vessel filled with all sorts of sharp objects, such as bent pins, iron nails, and thorns. They were also filled with what is known as a "taglock," which consists of items that tie a spell to an individual (Morningbird, 2023). This included hair and nail clippings. Finally, once the bottle was filled with these items, it would be topped up with urine, sealed, and embedded in the building they were meant to protect. It was thought that the urine would draw the witch to the bottle and that the sharp objects would cause her harm (Meier, 2019). Some witches nowadays still construct these bottles—yes, including with the urine—but, instead, bury them on the four corners of their property.

Sheela Na Gig

Sheela Na Gigs are, like the Roman fascinum, a strange and overtly sexual protective symbol. Essentially, Sheela Na Gigs were carvings found across Britain and Ireland that depicted an old woman squatting and pulling her vulva wide open. Even more oddly, they were found on Romanesque churches! The true meaning of them is lost to time, but it is theorized that because the Devil could not stand the sight of a woman's genitals, his presence would be driven away (Harding, 2016).

The Curious Case of Cats in Walls

It's important to say that the following is not a practice that I endorse! During the Medieval period, dried cats were often found within the structure of buildings, specifically the roofs. It is thought that they were meant to deter not only evil but also rat and mouse infestation. Indeed, sometimes, they were posed with rats or mice to depict their role more fully, as if displaying to any wandering pests just what the feline's spirit would do to them (*1196—Dried Cat,*

2021).

Four Thieves' Vinegar

This is a concoction of legend; it is said that during the time of the Black Death, there was a band of thieves who robbed victims of the plague but never got sick themselves. This was because they had created what is known as Four Thieves' Vinegar, which they carried on their person to smell as well as douse themselves in. While recipes for the mixture abound, none can be verified as the true, original recipe. In fact, some include the use of poisonous herbs, so any recipes found should be followed with the care that all herbal remedies should be dealt with—after all, just because they're natural doesn't mean they're safe (Kelley, 2020).

Amulets, Charms, and Talismans

Before I proceed with the rest of the book, and particularly the spells, it is important to delineate some parts of vocabulary that are frequently used within witchcraft communities. It can be difficult to get to grips with the differences between amulets, charms, and talismans at first, but as knowledge is power, it is definitely worth doing so.

These definitions, however, are complicated by the fact that different practitioners of magick will define these objects differently. The definitions I proffer here are from a couple of sources, showing some agreement with the basics of what these items are. These definitions are as follows (Auryn, 2020b; Webster, 2004):

- **Charm:** Any object that you carry with you that is imbued with a certain magickal purpose. This can be for protection, as we will cover here, but also for other things such as attracting love or bringing luck. This can be confusing because sometimes short magickal sayings are also called charms. Neither is incorrect, but when discussing them it is important to give context for what you are talking about.

- **Amulet:** An item crafted to ward off certain influences. Typically, this will be to protect the carrier or wearer.

- **Talisman:** An item crafted to bring in certain influences. With protection in mind, this may be to supplement and amplify one's magickal potency.

What this shows us is that all amulets and talismans are charms, but not all charms will be both amulets and talismans; they'll be one or the other, depending on their desired function.

It should be noted that, in his book on the matter, Nigel Pennick (2021) defines amulets as being formed from natural materials, whereas talismans carry with them inscriptions or symbols that relate to their purpose. While I do not delineate the items in the same way, these definitions show some of the ways that these items are made: sourcing a natural object and changing it in some way to conform to your magickal will.

The Evil Eye

It would be nigh on impossible to speak about the cultural and historical beliefs surrounding self-defense against magickal and psychic threats without talking about the evil eye.

As noted above, the nazar is the famous blue, white, and black stylized eye that is often itself erroneously called the evil eye but is, in fact, a ward against it. So, what is it? The actual evil eye is a psychic attack transferred by an envious look. Sometimes, this is thought to be conferred on purpose, but other times, it is thought to occur by accident, simply through looking at someone with jealousy in your heart. The consequences of the attack are wide-ranging—to the point of being thought to bring downfall to the person affected (Hargitai, 2018; Schwarcz, 2022; Volandes, 2020).

Belief in the evil eye spans a wide variety of cultures, from the southern Mediterranean all the way up to northern Europe and into Britain. Thoughts on this attack date back to the 6th century B.C.E, being referenced by many famous Classical authors—including Plato—but have survived even through the Christianization of Europe (Hargitai, 2018; King, 2016; Schwarcz, 2022; Volandes, 2020).

Fortunately, as well as having been written about as a risk to the successful and prosperous since this time, amulets designed to avert the evil eye also have a long history, hence the ubiquity of the nazar among tourist shops in Greece, Cyprus, and Turkey. I will cover a way to develop an amulet that can be adapted to protect against the evil eye in more detail in Chapter 5, although the egg divination and cleanse in the next chapter will also help.

Ethics and Responsibilities

It is always important to know your values. They will guide you through life, and that includes through your witchcraft practice as well. However, not everyone believes the same things. I have already spoken about how magick is amoral, meaning it has no moral value in and of itself. Instead, it is a tool that can be harnessed for any number of ends. How you choose to use your magick is entirely up to you.

That said, there is a lot of debate in witchcraft communities about the morality of certain spells. Those considered baneful—including some protection spells and return-to-sender spells—get the most attention along with love spells, which I won't cover here in detail for reasons of space and lack of relevance to the topic at hand. I will instead outline below the two most common perspectives on these ethical controversies. This will put you in good stead to consider these further and see where your personal views align. It is not my place to lecture you on either of these points: So long as you fully understand the consequences of your actions, you are free to make your choices according to your own personal set of ethics.

Wicca and the Threefold Law

In Wicca, perhaps the most famous religion featuring witchcraft, there are two doctrines that followers abide by. Firstly, there are the final two lines of the Wiccan Rede, the early version of which was written by famed witch Doreen Valiente in the 1960s. In the later, most quoted version, it states, "Eight words ye Wiccan Rede fulfill: An' it harm none, do what ye will" (Wigington, 2018c).

This is relatively easy to grasp, despite the stylistic choice of more Medieval language. The Rede is the basic guidance given to Wiccans, and it is summed up as allowing one to do whatever they wish, so long as it doesn't cause harm. This can be difficult to apply to life; as I stated previously, certain spells, even those considered to have "good" outcomes, will have unknown circumstances elsewhere. If you get a job, someone else doesn't. If you find money on the floor, it's fallen out of someone else's pocket. If you choose to follow the Rede, you must think through the possible consequences of your actions before acting and decide for yourself what "harm" here actually means.

The Threefold Law is the second part of the

Wiccan code of ethics. It is also mentioned in the Rede and is stated as, "Mind the Threefold Law ye should, three times bad and three times good" (Wigington, 2018c). What this essentially means is that the moral outcomes of your actions should be paid attention to because the energy you direct outwards comes back to you three times. There is debate over whether or not this means one hit that is three times stronger or three separate instances. However, the general view is that this is a reason to not harm others because to do so invites harm unto yourself.

Not everyone who practices witchcraft follows the Rede or even believes in the principle of the Threefold Law. There is an argument to be made that energy cannot be multiplied, and so cannot come back three times, although some who make this argument do concede that sometimes circumstances will rebound back onto the witch in question, particularly if they do not do their due diligence in protecting themselves when casting baneful magick. However, since the beginnings of Wicca, there has been a strong moral argument made that one should not cause harm to another, and many do believe in the power of this Law. Indeed, this is a commonality among many world religions.

With respect to protection magick, Wiccans are allowed to look out for themselves—indeed, it could be argued that they should protect themselves if they wish to cause harm to none because that includes the self, too. However, certain spell types will not be used by a Wiccan, such as more aggressive wards and return-to-sender spells. This is because they would cause harm to whoever wishes to hurt the witch, and they do not believe in causing harm to a person, regardless of their intentions.

As not all witches are Wiccan, belief in the Rede and the Law is not a prerequisite to practicing witchcraft. However, if Wicca is a practice that interests you, it is worth researching the Rede further and considering how you think it operates and how it should be followed.

Moral Relativism and Gray Witchcraft

Moral relativism is a train of thought in philosophy that essentially states that there is no such thing as a universal set of principles or ethics that one should abide by. It points out that many of the things we consider right or wrong actually inhere from our cultural perspective, which is a circumstance of birth. Some forms of moral relativism do note that some morals appear to be common among most cultures—such as murder being wrong—but even then, there may be nuances to how this is actually applied (*Moral Relativism*, 2022). For instance, many cultures will profess the evils of murder but will happily go to war, sending thousands to their deaths to cause injury to thousands of their enemies. Clearly, it isn't the killing that's decried but something else.

Many take the idea of moral relativism and apply it to reserving judgment about others' decisions—within reason, which will be limits applied by the individual reserving or dishing out the judgment. Many people also apply this to their own thoughts and actions, too. They argue that morality cannot be considered a static thing with hard and fast rules: Instead, the correct thing to do changes depending on the situation you find yourself in. Think, for example, about lying. Usually, we in Eurocentric cultures hold honesty in high regard, but when it comes to being asked by a friend, "Does my butt look big in this?" and it does, we'll often lie outright or fudge the truth a little to save their feelings.

This ties in with what is known as "gray witchcraft." As the author of *The Gray Witch's Grimoire, Amethyst Raine* (2012) explains that gray witchcraft is about balance. It does not shy away from or fear darkness, for it recognizes that this is simply the shadow cast by light. Following on from this, gray witches will use techniques that are called "white" and "black" magick in common parlance to create balance within the world. They do not follow the rule of harming none because, to them, it is sometimes necessary to harm a person in order to protect someone else.

This is applying moral relativism to magick. It essentially shows that, again, magick is a tool to be wielded by someone and applied based on their own moral code. For the gray witch, this means that ethics are looser, being applied depending on the situation at hand. Many gray witches do not believe in the Threefold Law, but some accept that they may face consequences for their actions in some way, usually if they are not properly prepared or protected. However, it is up to the practitioner to weigh up the pros and cons of any action before performing their magick, including any ramifications to themselves. If this is a risk they are willing to take in order to create balance or avert a negative situation, they will go ahead with the planned spell.

When it comes to protection magick, for the gray witch, anything is permitted so long as it keeps a balance. This means they may engage in what others would call a "tit-for-tat," using aggressive wards that bite back against unwanted interferences or using a return-to-sender spell to teach a would-be curser a lesson. All is dependent on their own assessment of what is required in a particular situation. For example, if another witch appears to be a serial hexer, the gray witch may decide it is high time they experience a taste of their own medicine. However, if a spirit is merely curious, they will behave in a more gentle manner towards it when trying to remove its influence over a space.

Free Will and Coercion

Another concept that comes up a lot when discussing magickal ethics is free will. Many people who believe in the Wiccan Rede will say that anything is permitted so long as a person's free will is not impinged. Some witches who perform baneful magick will take a similar line when it comes to targeted love spells. This is because setting a spell upon someone in particular with the aim of causing them to love you means that you are altering their free will because you are forcing them to do something they otherwise didn't want to do.

For many, this is where they draw the line in their ethics, as they believe consent is necessary to perform magick—and even apply this to other, beneficial spells, such as healing, not wanting to do them for other people without their knowledge. Others do not mind doing any sort of spell; indeed, some make a career out of doing them.

Free will and harm can be tricky to discern the moral boundaries of. While you may not wish to impinge on someone's agency, there are circumstances where this may be ideal. For example, if someone is behaving in an abusive or harmful way, binding their actions will stop their behavior at the cost of their free will, but if it's the only way to prevent greater harm, a morally relativist gray witch may take this action. Again, the issue of free will is something to consider for your own witchcraft practice.

Karma

Ah, karma: a word thrown about a lot when talking about spiritual ethics, but one which is deeply misunderstood. Many people talk about karma as the consequences of someone's actions in this life. You'll often hear people say of a harmful person that karma will bite them in the butt at some point. It is treated as the "just desserts" someone gets based on their good or bad behavior.

However, the concept of karma originally comes from Indian philosophy in religions such as Hinduism and Buddhism. As the latter, in particular, has spread out across the world, many of us have learned this word but misconstrued it. Karma, instead of being the thing delivered upon you in this life, is the law that governs what your existence will be like in the next life. You almost accrue it by the actions you carry out in this life, good or bad, and then, when it comes to being reincarnated—an important concept in these religions—karma determines the many different circumstances that you will be born into. As such, it is a call to live life morally—according to the precepts of the religion in question—as well as an explanation for why your life is how it currently is (Olivelle, 2023).

You can be a witch and believe in karma; indeed, many pagans believe in some kind of reincarnation, and so, the belief in karma may make sense to you in terms of how certain lives are allotted to certain souls. However, it is important to know what it actually is, otherwise, we are doing the cherrypicking and bastardizing of cultures that I warned about in the introduction to this book. It is always good to be mindful of this and to use the proper terms. While you may believe that the energy people give out comes back to them in this life in some way, it is better to say that than to misuse a term with a very specific meaning dating back hundreds of years, debated thoroughly within a deep philosophical tradition.

CHAPTER 2
IDENTIFYING CURSES, HEXES, AND PSYCHIC ATTACKS

In Witchcraft, each of us must reveal our own truth. — Starhawk

Before you can even start thinking about reversal magick, you've got to first figure out what exactly it is you're reversing.

This information will put you in good stead for the remaining chapters of the book. You must be clear on what it is you're trying to prevent, reverse, or banish before doing any magick as you always want to be precise in your casting. This is because it is better to direct your energy to one point at a time, rather than throwing it out willy-nilly, as you will then have more control over the consequences of the spell and its efficacy can be measured more easily.

You should always first rule out mundane influence—that is, the non-magickal—before jumping to the conclusion that you are the victim of baneful magick or psychic attack. This will be covered more below in the section *Distinguishing Between Natural Events and Magickal Interference*. This is because, fortunately, it is much more likely for an "attack" to actually be something non-supernatural instead.

However, if after this analysis, you are still concerned that you have come under attack in some way, you'll need to know what sort of attack it is. This is what I will cover in the first section below, as there is indeed a difference between curses, hexes, and jinxes, as well as psychic attacks from elsewhere. I'll then outline what the warning signs of these types of attack are so that you can be aware of them should they come about. Finally, after a trip down the lane of discernment, I'll cover the ways that you can find out, through divination, if you have indeed been attacked, ending with an understanding of the longer-term effects of these psychic injuries.

Curses, Hexes, Jinxes, and Psychic Attacks: What's the Difference?

It can be a bit confusing to discern the differences between psychic and magickal attacks, particularly because they can share symptoms and effects.

However, there is indeed a difference between curses, hexes, and jinxes—which are magickal attacks—and psychic attacks. Knowing what sort of attack you have come under allows you to reverse it much more easily. In some cases, a simple cleansing of yourself or a space will be required, whereas others may warrant a more labor-intensive spell to undo their influence. Knowing what is necessary prevents you from expending too much of your own energy on ineffective and inefficient actions.

Curses, Hexes, and Jinxes

Let's first talk about the similarities between curses, hexes, and jinxes. All of these can be called "baneful" magick, meaning that they are cast with malicious intent to harm. As Glinda Porter (2021) writes, it is impossible to perform any of these unintentionally— to confer any of these effects in such a way would instead be considered a psychic attack. This is because any of these actions are spells, which require the intent and focused energetic exertion of the caster.

Another similarity is that all of these spells can be placed on not just individuals but also groups, places, and objects. We often hear stories about places carrying a curse if one disrespects it, such as a graveyard, and there are often urban legends about cursed dolls and suchlike. While it is likely to be more common to send these sorts of spells against an individual or their family, it is worth bearing these similarities in mind.

When it comes to the differences, however, we can speak in terms of how "serious" the injury caused by the spell is and how long it lasts. The blog Tea and Rosemary outlines this well, and so, the information below is, in part, based on their account of these (*Curses, hexes, and jinxes: What's the difference?*, 2020).

A jinx is a short-lived spell that is relatively harmless, causing minor annoyance. For example, you could cast a spell on someone so that they keep stubbing their toe on any table they walk past for a day or send them nightmares one night.

A hex is more harmful and lasts somewhat longer than a jinx. Often, a caster will set it to last until the person who's been hexed has learned their lesson, whatever that may be. The longest it will last is perhaps a whole season. An example of a hex would be to cause the individual to ruminate on and regret their actions, particularly if it was a spell to get justice, as many hexes nowadays are. Another example may be to cause ruin in one specific area of their life. Social media sites like TikTok abound with videos of hexes performed to remove someone's sexual prowess, for want of a better, PG-13 term, usually as an act of revenge.

A curse, however, is the most harmful of all and can last a lifetime—sometimes even longer, if we're discussing generational curses. The harm caused can be absolutely dire; indeed, there are many folktales and urban legends of curses causing someone to die in a tragic way. The impact of each curse will vary, but we can get an idea of them via some examples, such as a curse to destroy all hopes of a relationship or career or a curse to return the hurt caused by a person onto themselves. This is another reason why these spells are sometimes used for a sense of justice; there is much talk in online witch communities of cursing abusers, for instance.

Because curses are used in the worst-case scenario, they are quite rare. Most of the spells we hear about as "curses" are in fact a hex or even "just" a jinx. This will have an impact on how we will go about dismantling such spells, as less energy and focus are required to break a hex than a full-blown curse.

Types of Psychic Attack

The College of Psychic Studies notes, "it is probable that we have each experienced a psychic attack at some point in our life, whether we are aware of it or not" (*What Is a Psychic Attack?*, 2022). This is because psychic attacks, unlike baneful magick, can be performed unintentionally. An example of this, the evil eye, was covered in the last chapter, wherein we saw that many cultures believe psychic attacks to often be unintentionally cast by a jealous gaze.

So, what is a psychic attack? Essentially, there are two kinds: Firstly, it can be the conference of negative energy from one person to another, as we see in the evil eye example. The second kind is the sapping of energy from one being into another. We see this in the example of what are called "energy" or "psychic vampires," who may not even know themselves to be one but still "feed" from the energy of others (Konstantinos, 2002).

It is easier to psychically attack those we are close with because we already share some form of energetic bond (*What Is a Psychic Attack?*, 2022). Again, this is frequently unintentional: Discussing intense emotions can be draining, but that doesn't mean we should neglect the emotional needs of our loved ones and not comfort them when they're down. Instead, we can use a shield to protect our energy from becoming drained during these situations, something I cover in Chapter 4.

This is particularly important for those who are empaths—people who feel the emotions of another person and know exactly what they're feeling because of this. While being an empath can be an amazing gift, it also often results in quite a bit of fatigue. If this is you, it is very important to learn how to shield and perhaps create a protective amulet in order to conserve your own energy.

A psychic attack tends not to last very long, and we will typically regain this energy ourselves over a period of time. We can help ourselves to regain energy by cleansing, grounding through connection to the earth and heavenly bodies' energy, and doing restful activities. We'll cover these more in the fourth chapter.

Nonhuman Causes of Psychic Attacks

It is not only other humans who can threaten our energy, however. We share our world with a variety of different autonomous spirits and entities, both human and nonhuman. Most are happy to live and let live, getting on with their own lives and not bothering us unless we choose to try and contact them ourselves. They're like other people with their own business going on, essentially.

Some entities, on the other hand, do actively engage with us, particularly if we have (perhaps latent) psychic abilities or practice witchcraft. Many of these spirits will be helpful, wanting to work with you to achieve your magickal goals and teach you more so that you advance along your path. These are commonly called "spirit guides," and such relationships can be incredibly meaningful. Unfortunately, however, a very small minority of spirits do not have kind intentions and so may decide to take it upon themselves to inflict psychic damage against a witch.

I cannot emphasize enough that this is a very rare occurrence indeed. Tales of demonic possession and poltergeists wreaking havoc in a house are almost always explained by mundane causes, of which there are many. However, as this book aims at being a comprehensive guide to self-defensive magick, it is only right to mention the rare and the weird so that you have a well-rounded knowledge of psychic and magickal threats. It is beyond the scope of this book to delve deeper into the types of entities known to occasionally cause chaos, but suffice it to say it isn't just demons—indeed, it very, very rarely is. However, it is possible to do further research into this if it is an area that interests you. That said, what I can cover in the space of this book are techniques to protect yourself from unwanted spirits, as well as the basics of banishing. Both of these topics will be covered in later chapters.

The Signs of Hexes and Psychic Attacks

Because hexes and curses can target a number of different things, the possible signs of them are quite vast. Psychic attacks can also vary. However, all of these have some similarities in the form of the most common symptoms they bring. These are (*What Is a Psychic Attack?*, 2022; *"Am I cursed?" 10 symptoms of magickal danger,* n.d.; Thorne, 2022)

- extended bouts of ongoing bad luck or failure in one specific area of life
- becoming more accident-prone or more accidents happening around you for an ongoing period of time
- lack of energy
- depression, erratic mood, and suicidal thoughts, when this is unusual for you

- chronic health issues that have no known medical cause, such as joint pain, headaches, and frequent nausea
- stress for no apparent reason
- vivid, recurring nightmares
- sexual dysfunction of some kind or another
- feeling uncomfortable in certain places, especially if they are also avoided by children or pets
- strange, unexplainable happenings in the home, such as pictures falling off the wall or your keys being moved about
- relationship difficulties and repeated arguments, including with partners, family, and friends, with no apparent cause—just tension and conflict arising easily, with quick, heated tempers
- people avoiding you or becoming more indifferent to you
- decreased creativity, particularly if one is usually a creative sort
- uncharacteristic compulsions to do certain things, or acting out of character, in general
- bad omens`

Distinguishing Between Natural Events and Magickal Interference

As you will notice, many of the above symptoms of magickal and psychic attacks could have perfectly rational explanations. There is a saying that gets passed around quite a lot in witchcraft communities: "Mundane over magickal." This means that we should always look first for causes that are non-magickal which could explain certain phenomena. Another way of putting it might be "don't jump to (magickal) conclusions."

More often than not, with some thinking about the phenomena you are experiencing, there will be a material cause. This is because things like magickal attacks, hauntings, and ongoing psychic attacks are all quite rare phenomena. While it is wonderful to experience the magickal in our everyday lives and see the vast interconnectedness of the universe and its inhabitants, we should be wary of assigning occult meaning to everything because this can lead down a tricky road of paranoia, among other problems.

So, how do you go about discerning whether or not your experiences are caused by magick? Well, depending on what's going on for you, the questions you need to ask yourself will be different. Below is an inexhaustive list of the sorts of questions you may need to ask yourself. These may then break down into even more questions, but it is important to follow these lines of inquiry so that you have fully ruled out all logical explanations. Some of the questions you may ask are as follows:

- Is there a medical explanation for my physical

or emotional symptoms? To fully explore this option, you will need to go to an actual doctor or other medical professional trained in the area of your particular issue.

- Have I been exposing myself to too much stress? Consider whether or not you are coping well with your responsibilities, if you are trying to fit too much into your days, or if anything has happened recently that could be causing anxiety, fatigue, or other symptoms.

- Is this really out of the ordinary? Some things may seem strange, but when we think about them in more detail, we begin to see that actually they're quite normal. An example of this, to make it clearer, is seeing a particular type of bird associated with a deity regularly and, at first, thinking it is a sign, until you realize it is because of the migratory or mating patterns of that species at that time of year.

- Is this really happening that much more than usual? Consider the frequency and duration of the phenomena you have been experiencing. It could simply be confirmation bias: Once an idea has popped into your head, you begin to notice it everywhere and think it's more common than it is because you simply didn't notice it before.

- Could this be caused by carbon monoxide poisoning or other environmental factors? It might sound strange, but carbon monoxide leaking into an environment can cause all sorts of strange symptoms, and a cursory internet search pulls up multiple instances of it being the source of what were thought to be hauntings.

- Did this happen suddenly or has it been brewing for some time? This might equally apply to a variety of different phenomena, from a progressive worsening of health to the dissolution of a relationship.

- Could this be the result of unresolved trauma? Spiritual bypassing is a psychological defense mechanism that prevents us from having to deal with hard truths about ourselves by assigning a magickal cause to certain symptoms and phenomena when, in fact, the cause is unresolved issues and traumas. If you think this is the case, consider delving into this in more detail, potentially with the support of a mental health professional such as a trustworthy therapist.

- Am I a forgetful person who lives with other people, and so, might that be why it seems things keep moving by themselves? You may very well be forgetting where you put your keys, or you keep leaving them in strange places where your roomies will find and move them.

- Has my child, family member, pet, or other loved one experienced something recently that could have caused them to behave in this way? Fireworks and loud storms may make pets frightened—and sometimes children, too. Family members may be going through stresses of their own and so may act out of character. There may also be underlying health issues to consider—another reason why it may be good to consult a medical or veterinary specialist.

Using Divination to Uncover Hidden Curses, Hexes, and Attacks

Divination isn't just about trying to predict what the future may hold. It can also be used to uncover hidden information. Because of this, you can use it to find out if you are under attack in some way. Before introducing some ways to do this, however, I should make two points.

Firstly, you don't need to be psychic in the sense of common parlance to use divination methods like those listed below. While being claircognizant—able to know, without mundane means, information that you would not otherwise know—would be extremely handy in this and other scenarios, it is not essential for divination. Tools to connect to the energies that surround us and are within us will mean you can uncover the necessary information. However, if you are still worried about your abilities, you can find a (reputable) reader of various methods online to commission a reading.

Secondly, because a lot is at stake when it comes to psychic or magickal attack, it would be a good idea to double-check any readings, preferably using different methods. In these situations, it is good to try a "yes/no" means of answering questions as well as one that is more descriptive—for example, a pendulum reading backed up by Tarot, which I explain below. This will mean that you'll be able to better discern the accuracy of the reading and know for certain what has transpired. You may also double-check by asking someone else to perform a reading for you.

With all that said, I'll now go through three of the more common ways of divining for hexes and psychic attacks. This is not an exhaustive list, however. If you find another divinatory system more helpful, then I would say to use that. Everyone's ability to tap into their intuition is different, and so, different methods word better for different people.

Pendulum

Pendulums are often crystals hanging from a chain, but anything that hangs can be used as a pendulum, whether that's a treasured ring dangling from a necklace or a stone with a hole in it attached to some string. They are popular for all sorts of questions that can be answered with a yes or no, although there are ways to get a "maybe" from them too.

There are a couple of ways to divine with a

pendulum. The easiest is with a pendulum board. These can be found cheaply online or created at home. You would plot out a circle divided up into eighths. One line (usually the vertical) would have "yes" at either end, another "no" (usually the horizontal), and the remaining ones would be "maybe" and "ask again." You can then dangle the pendulum steadily over the board and ask your questions, using the movements to come to your answer.

Another way—one that does not rely on a board—is to capture the pendulum's natural calibrations (Thorne, 2020). To do this, you would ask the pendulum to show you how it moves for each answer. You would then test this with questions you already know the answer to, such as "Is my name X?" "Am I a woman?" or "Do I live in X town?". Once you are certain you have ascertained how the pendulum moves for each possible answer, you may proceed to ask it yes/no questions about your current malady to find out what ails you.

Tarot and Oracle Cards

Not all oracle cards are Tarot, but all Tarot could be called a type of oracle card, for these are decks of cards containing symbols that, when interpreted, can tell you more meaningful and nuanced answers than is possible with a pendulum.

Cartomancy—as divination by cards is called—is decades old and a very popular means to uncover information. Tarot is the most famous of these cartomancy methodologies. Composed of a deck of 78 cards, it started off during the early modern period as a game, but by the 1780s, it came to be adapted for fortune-telling (Parlett, 1999). The most famous imagery for Tarot is those derived from the Rider Waite Smith deck, created at the turn of the 20th century and popular to this day (*The Rider Waite Smith Deck,* n.d.).

It is well beyond the scope of this book to go into the meanings of the various cards, but there are many books and online resources for this—indeed, as I said previously, I have written one myself (Visconti, 2019). However, it is possible to outline here a spread that will be of use when divining about attacks. A spread is when cards are laid out in a specific order relating to certain questions, with the cards then interrogated individually according to how the symbolism answers the question; this is then analyzed to see the relationship between cards and what this says about the situation as a whole.

A simple three-card layout that is a standard one in a Tarot reader's roster is as follows: Laid out in a horizontal line, the first card represents the source of a problem, the second its effect, and the third its solution. Check the meaning of the card for each question, sure, but also try to come to your own understanding of the answer. What does the card intuitively feel like it is telling you? What is the symbolism of the card saying? Its colors, layout, and motifs? Take some time to ponder the cards, and write down your interpretation so that you do not forget it. The benefits of this spread are that it can give you an idea of how to rid yourself of the current problem on top of confirming if you are under a spell or psychic attack.

Oomancy: Divination With Eggs

A previously fairly unheard-of method of divination, oomancy—divination using eggs (yes, you read that correctly)—has exploded in popularity due to discussions on social media sites such as TikTok. Combining both a form of divining about curses as well as a way to cleanse and remove them, the method is known within the Latine Brujería community as *"limpia."* However, similar rituals can be found in other folk magick traditions.

Eggs work for this because they are considered empty vessels (Alejandrez-Prasad, 2023). The ritual can remove curses in some instances because the egg absorbs it, but even if the curse requires another spell to break it, the egg will be able to tell if there is a hex present.

So, how do you do it? First, fetch your egg, a cup with some cold, salted water or incense for cleansing in it, an empty, clear cup, and a candle, and find a place where you'll be able to concentrate. Then, there are several stages involved in this ritual, which I will lay out step-by-step (Alejandrez-Prasad, 2023):

1. Pray your intentions over the egg while holding it. Fill it with your energy to connect with it while telling it what you need it to do. Invoke a deity if you so wish (something I'll cover more in Chapter 3).
2. Cleanse the egg. You can use the salt water for this or smoke cleanse it by waving protective incense all around it (I'll cover protective herbs in Chapter 3, too, and cleansing in Chapter 4).
3. Fill the empty cup to about 75% full of cold water, and light your candle.
4. Run the egg over your entire body, top to bottom. Do so gently, so as not to crack it. Do this several times, until you feel intuitively that you have done enough. You may repeat your intentions or pray as you do this.
5. Crack your egg into the cup, and place the eggshell to one side. Take photos so that you can refer back to them if necessary.
6. Read the egg using the interpretations below.
7. Dispose of the egg—not in the trash, but either down the sink or flushed down the toilet.

To read the egg, you will need to consider how it sits in the water. There are many ways it may hold up in the fluid. Interpretations of these are as follows (Alejandrez-Prasad, 2023; Brethauer, 2023):

- **Bubbles:** Small bubbles signify a successful

cleanse, whereas big ones suggest gossip and being watched.

- **Foam:** There are things brewing beneath the surface that you are currently unaware of. Further divination may prove useful here.
- **Cloudiness:** Cloudiness like a gray mist over the yolk represents physical symptoms that require focus and must be lifted.
- **Water remains clear:** Things are going well— no need to be concerned!
- **Strings:** These come top-to-bottom and represent "cords" connecting you to others that need to be cut. They may also represent worries, particularly if there are many of them and you are feeling anxious. Basically, they are signs of negative energy still affecting you.
- **Cages:** These enclose the yolk, are big, and are usually egg-shaped themselves. They symbolize feeling closed in and trapped.
- **Spikes:** These come bottom-to-top and represent negative energy being released.
- **Cobwebs:** General negativity that we pick up in our day-to-day lives. A simple cleanse should do the trick.
- **An eye:** The evil eye has been placed upon you and needs to be removed.
- **A face:** This represents someone who has cursed you.
- **Other symbols:** Sometimes, you may see

other, rarer symbols in the egg, which can be also interpreted; guides for symbols can be bought or found online—something relating to dreams or tea leaf readings would be helpful.

- **Egg shell in glass:** Be sure this isn't just because you cracked the egg badly! However, if there is shell, it can reveal that the situation is overwhelming even the ritual and will require further action.

- **Blood in the yolk:** Something needs to be healed, or a hex needs to be broken. Consider further divination to find out what it is, exactly.

- **Yolk doesn't sink to the bottom:** A symbol of a curse or attack of some kind.

- **Broken yolk:** There is an attack or negativity against you that has "broken open" and is currently having an effect on you. It will need to be released.

- **Double yolk:** A good omen! While it can mean twins, it is generally a sign of prosperity (due to the connection to fertility).

As you can see, sometimes, the egg itself is sufficiently cleansing on its own to rid you of negativity. However, it can also reveal a need for further investigation—hence my call to you to always double-check—or further action. This is what I will cover in the following chapters, after taking a brief detour to talk about the building blocks necessary to construct and carry out spells, such as what herbs and crystals correspond to protection.

CHAPTER 3
TOOLS AND INGREDIENTS FOR REVERSAL AND PROTECTION SPELLS

You are the most powerful tool in your life. Use your energy, your thoughts, and your magick wisely! – Dacha Avalin

Before it is possible to look at means of protection, reversal, and banishing, it is necessary to understand the elements that will comprise these spells. Different ingredients will correspond to different magickal ends. "Correspondence" here means the properties of a herb, crystal, oil, or other ingredient in relation to its magickal uses. It is also pertinent to understand the importance of timing in your spell work because different moon phases and days of the week have different properties, too. As well as this, I will run through the most common tools used in witchcraft so that you know what sort of things you should gradually build a collection of. Finally, although it is possible to have a secular witchcraft practice, many people choose to work with deities, spirits, and ancestors in their craft, so I'll go through the basics of this, too. However, it is good to first understand the roles of the different elements in witchcraft.

The Use of Elements

Most witchcraft in the West uses the classical four elements as a basis for their craft. These are earth, air, fire, and water. They have the four cardinal directions mapped to them: North is earth, east is air, fire is south, and water is west. Many witches will use a compass to place their working altar in one of the directions for different spells according to what they are trying to achieve so that they are facing the appropriate direction when working their magick. This is because each element rules over different aspects of life (Beyer, 2019; Saint Thomas, 2020; Wigington, 2019b):

- **Earth:** Associated with fertility and prosperity, earth is a very stable element that relates strongly to the materiality of the world around us. In Tarot, it rules over the Suit of Pentacles (sometimes called the Suit of Coins). In astrology, it rules over the signs Taurus, Virgo, and Capricorn. In alchemical terms, it is cold and dry, as well as carrying feminine or receptive energies. It is associated with the colors green and brown.

- **Air:** Corresponding to all areas of communication, air is associated with the rational mind. In astrology, it rules over Aquarius, Libra, and Gemini. In Tarot, it is associated with the Suit of Swords. In alchemical terms, it is warm and moist and carries masculine or active energies. It is associated with the color yellow.

- **Fire:** Associated with protection and all kinds of strength and courage, fire relates to the will. In alchemy, it is warm and dry and also carries masculine or active energy. In astrology, it rules over Aries, Leo, and Sagittarius, and in Tarot, the Suit of Wands. It is associated with the colors orange and red.

- **Water:** Healing, cleansing, and purifying, water rules over emotions and intuition. In astrology, it commands Pieces, Cancer, and Scorpio, and it is associated with the Suit of Cups in Tarot. It is moist and cold in alchemy, as well as carrying feminine or receptive energies. It is associated with the color blue.

There is one more element to consider, however: spirit. This fifth element is sometimes also known as "ether" or "quintessence." It does not have formalized correspondences as the other elements do, but it is instead the energy or essence that suffuses everything in the universe and connects us with what is around us. It also helps us to connect with the spiritual realms

(Beyer, 2019).

You might even say that it is the manipulation of the spirit within us, our ingredients, and the wider world that allows magick to work. This is, of course, just a theory—as there is no singularly known way to understand the workings of magick—but one that many practitioners subscribe to.

However, we don't necessarily invoke spirit as we do many of the other elements. With these, they are frequently called to help with magick in a process known as "calling in the quarters." There are many different mythical beings that have associations with different elements, including archangels, the fae, and elementals. There are also those known as the Watchtowers or the Guardians of the elements. Traditionally, they are called upon in Wiccan ways of laying a magickal circle during spell work or ritual—something we cover in a more simple, accessible form in Chapter 5. However, suffice it to say that you can invoke the powers of the elements in your magick if you so wish to add potency to your spells. One way to do this is by figuring out what element a herb relates to, as different plants have been ascribed different elemental energies based on their appearance. This practice can be included in protection magick.

The Tools of the Trade

There are a number of tools that are common in witchcraft that it is important to familiarize yourself with. Many of these are used for ritual purposes in religions like Wicca, but they also each serve both magickal and practical functions and act as powerful symbols for certain concepts. The common tools of the witch are as follows (Alexander, 2014; Chamberlain, 2017b):

- **Wand:** Yes, magick isn't about fairytale witches, but the notion of a magick wand had to come from somewhere; the wand is indeed a common tool of witches. Wands are used to draw down and direct energy during spell casting and can be used when casting magickal circles, which I will go into more detail about in Chapter 5. Wands correspond to the element of fire. Traditionally, the wand is made from wood, but nowadays, it can be fashioned from a variety of materials, including crystal. Many witches will find their own wand in nature— not by cutting wood from a tree, which would be impolite unless the tree's spirit agrees to it, but by sourcing sticks from the ground. While it is not essential, many wands are also customized by the owner, such as with carvings of runes and sigils.

- **Athame:** A blunt ritual dagger, traditionally double-sided and with a black handle, the athame is also used for directing energy. Sometimes, it is used for cutting through energy. It is associated with the element air.

- **Pentacle:** A symbol associated with Wicca as a religion but also with the element earth in magick, in general, the pentacle is a five-pointed star—one point at the top—with a circle around it; it is a pentagram if it is without the circle. In magick, it is used for charging items and is also a potent symbol of protection itself.

- **Chalice:** Associated quite naturally with the element water, the chalice is a vessel dedicated to holding liquids for ritual activity. In Wicca, it is common to end magickal and ritual practices with some food and drink (traditionally small cakes and ale), and so, this is the most common use for chalices. However, you may use a specially demarcated tea cup if a spell requires the drinking of a herbal tea—and always remember to use herbs safely!

- **Cauldron:** Also associated with the element water, a cauldron should be made from a fire-resistant material (traditionally iron) and have a lid that can smother flames if necessary. It is used to safely burn incense or spell materials.

While you don't need to run out straight away and amass all of the tools listed above, it is worth knowing what the most common ones are in witchcraft and gradually building up your collection of these. When you first begin, it is enough to use what is at hand, but over time, it is nice to gather together items specifically only used as tools of magick. This helps you to draw a demarcation between everyday life and the sacred, bringing you closer to your craft when you engage with these objects and making it easier to enter into a mindset conducive to casting magick.

Essential Herbs, Crystals, and Oils for Defense

Spells almost always need ingredients. Like the elements, each ingredient has its own correspondences—properties that can be drawn on to affect the change you want to see in the world. By working with these ingredients in your spell, you can harness their energy to supplement your own, shaping it with your intention toward your desired end. This will become clearer in the later chapters.

For now, let's take a look at some herbs and crystals that correspond to the intentions you'll have around protection, cleansing, banishing, and hex-breaking. Once this is done, I will then discuss how oils can be used safely as a different means of harnessing the power of herbs.

Herbs

Below are some common and easy-to-obtain herbs that can be used in defensive magick. A word of caution, however: You should not ingest or burn any herb without first doing your due diligence on whether or not it is safe. While herbs are the bounty of nature, this does not mean they are always safe to work with in every way. There are many guides available about this online or in books.

As well as their magickal properties, I will include some other information about other associations you can draw on. I'll list the feminine/receptive or masculine/projective properties, what element the plant is associated with, and what planet they are associated with, as this is one way to bring different forms of energy into your work by drawing on celestial and elemental power.

Some herbs you may begin to work with once you've done your due diligence are as follows (Cunningham, 2007):

- **Aloe vera:** A feminine/receptive plant associated with the moon and the element water. It is used for protection.
- **Ash:** A fiery plant that is masculine/protective and associated with the sun. It is used for protection.
- **Basil:** A masculine/projective, fiery plant associated with Mars and used for protection and banishing.
- **Bay/Laurel:** Another fiery masculine/projective plant used for protection, cleansing, banishing, and hex-breaking.
- **Beans:** Associated with air and the planet Mercury, beans are all masculine/projective

and can be used for protection and banishing.

- **Birch:** A watery, feminine/receptive plant, birch is associated with the planet Venus. It can be used for cleansing, banishing, and protection.

- **Cactus:** The associations of cacti vary due to them being a classification of plants, but all can have their spines used for protection.

- **Cedar:** Another fiery masculine/projective tree associated with the sun, it can be used for cleansing and protection.

- **Chamomile:** A watery masculine/projective plant that can be used for many things, such as protection, cleansing, and hex-breaking.

- **Chili:** Unsurprisingly associated with fire, chili peppers are ruled by the planet Mars and are masculine/projective. They can be used for hex-breaking.

- **Cinnamon:** Yet another projective/masculine plant associated with fire and, this time, the sun, cinnamon is used for protection.

- **Clove:** A masculine/projective plant associated with fire and the planet Jupiter, it can be used for banishing and protection.

- **Coconut:** A feminine/receptive plant, coconut is associated with water and the moon, and it can be used for cleansing and protection.

- **Cotton:** Another feminine/receptive plant associated with the moon, this plant corresponds with the earth element, and it can be used for protection.

- **Cumin:** This masculine/projective herb, cumin, is associated with Mars and fire. It is used for protection and banishing.

- **Dragon's Blood:** A resin commonly used in incense blends, you can probably already infer from Dragon's Blood's name that it'll be a fiery plant. It is also masculine/projective and associated with Mars. You can draw on its power for protection and banishing.

- **Eucalyptus:** A feminine/receptive plant associated with water and the moon. It can be used for protection.

- **Fern:** Associated with Mercury and air, ferns are also projective/masculine in their energies. They are used for protection and banishing.

- **Frankincense:** We're back to fire and the sun with frankincense. It, too, is masculine/projective and used for protection, banishing, and cleansing.

- **Garlic:** A projective/masculine plant, garlic is fiery and associated with Mars. It is used for protection and banishing.

- **Geranium:** A watery plant associated with Venus, it is feminine/receptive. It is used for protection.

- **Heather:** Another feminine/receptive plant associated with water and Venus, it can be used for protection.

- **Holly:** A masculine/projective plant associated with Mars and fire, it is used for protection.

- **Ivy:** A feminine/receptive plant, ivy is associated with water and Saturn. It is used for protection.

- **Juniper:** Associated with the sun, fire, and masculine/projective energies, juniper is used for banishing and protection.

- **Lavender:** A masculine/projective plant associated with air and the planet Mercury, lavender is used for protection and cleansing.

- **Lemon:** Another feminine/receptive plant, lemon is associated with water and the moon; lemon can be used for cleansing.

- **Lime:** Associated with the sun, lime is fiery and masculine/projective. It is used for protection and hex-breaking.

- **Marjoram:** A masculine/projective yet airy plant associated with Mercury. Marjoram can be used for protection.

- **Mugwort:** Another feminine/receptive plant, mugwort is associated with Venus and the element earth. It is used for protection.

- **Nettle:** Back to masculine/projective, now. As anyone who has been stung by a nettle will not be surprised to learn, it is associated with fire and the planet Mars. It is excellent at protection, hex-breaking, and banishing.

- **Oak:** A fiery tree that is both masculine/projective and associated with the sun, it is used for protection.
- **Olive:** Associated with the fiery sun, olive is also masculine/projective and used for protection.
- **Onion:** Masculine/projective and fiery, onion is associated with Mars and used for protection and banishing.
- **Parsley:** An airy plant associated with Mercury, parsley is masculine/projective, too. It is used for protection and cleansing.
- **Peony:** A masculine/projective plant associated with fire and the sun, it can be used for banishing and projection.
- **Pepper:** Unsurprisingly fiery, pepper is masculine/projective and also associated with Mars. It is used for protection, hex-breaking, and cleansing.
- **Peppermint:** Associated with fire but also the planet Mercury, peppermint is masculine/projective and good for cleansing.
- **Pine:** An airy plant associated with Mars, pine is a masculine/projective ingredient useful for protection, cleansing, and banishing.
- **Rice:** Another plant related to air, but this time sun, rice is also masculine/projective. It can be used for protection.

- **Rose:** A feminine/receptive plant unsurprisingly associated with Venus and water, rose—in particular, its thorns—can be used for protection.
- **Rosemary:** Good for protection, banishing, and cleansing, rosemary is a fiery Mars-linked plant that is projective/masculine.
- **Garden sage:** Associated with Jupiter and the element air, sage is a masculine/projective plant used for protection and cleansing. This should not be confused with white sage, the use of which is a closed Indigenous practice.
- **Sandalwood (white):** Back to a feminine/receptive plant, sandalwood is associated with water and the moon. It is used for banishing and protection.
- **Thistle:** Used for hex-breaking, protection, banishing, and cleansing, thistle is a projective/masculine plant. It is associated with fire and Mars.
- **Thyme:** A feminine/receptive plant associated with Venus and water, it can be used for cleansing.
- **Valerian:** A watery plant associated with Venus, it is feminine/receptive and used for protection and cleansing.
- **Vervain:** A receptive/feminine plant associated with Venus and earth, vervain is used for cleansing, banishing, and protection.

You don't need to rush out and buy all these herbs at once. However, this should act as a short guide to some herbs you can use in rituals and spells and allow you to substitute one for another if need be. You can also do more research into the uses of these herbs historically, within folk magick, and within herbalism to find out more about them.

Crystals

As with the above, this is but a list for beginners to become acquainted with some of the crystals and rocks that you can use in your defensive magick and is in no way supposed to be totally comprehensive. Again, each one of these stones can be researched further, and you needn't rush out to buy them all immediately. Small chips and tumble stones can, however, be purchased at low prices and will work just as well as that great, big, several-hundred-dollar hunk of quartz. So, without further ado, here is a short list of protective gems (Cunningham, 2021):

- agate (banded, black, and brown)
- amethyst
- carnelian.
- clear quartz
- coral
- flint
- garnet
- jade
- jet
- lapis lazuli

- malachite
- marble
- obsidian
- onyx
- petrified wood
- pumice
- red jasper
- sunstone
- tiger's eye
- tourmaline (red and black)
- turquoise

Additionally, the use of stones can be implemented in many ways. For instance, aquamarine can be used for purification and pumice for banishment.

The Safe and Proper Use of Oils

People sometimes have a perception that everything natural is harmless. I've already cautioned against ingesting and burning herbs you are unfamiliar with because this widespread belief simply isn't the case. These words of warning also apply to essential oils, which are created by condensing the oils of a plant down to create a chemical that can be harmful if not used correctly.

I am not trying to scare you off from using essential oils, however. There are ways to do this safely, and many witches find them useful in their craft. You can create oil blends yourself quite safely at home to use in magick, typically for anointing the self or consecrating ritual objects.

So, it is perfectly possible to add essential oils into your practice safely. Here is some advice on how to do so (Wilson, 2019):

- Dilute all oils in a carrier oil; you can even correspond these to your magickal intentions, so olive would work well here for protection. The percentage of essential oil should not exceed 5% of the total mixture. For reference, six drops to one ounce of carrier oil gives a dilution of 1%.

- Before applying topically, check that the oil is safe to do so, particularly with certain health conditions and medications.

- Like with hair dye, if you mean to apply the oil to yourself or another person, do a patch test first by applying a small amount to the crook of your elbow and observing its effect for 24 hours before washing it off. If there is no reaction, you are good to go.

- Never ingest essential oils or apply them on mucous membranes. They can wreak havoc with your insides.

- Only diffuse oils in a well-ventilated place, and only for around 20–30 minutes at a time.

- Be aware that some oils in the air are harmful to children and pets. Research the safety of your oils before diffusing them.

- Keep out of reach of children and pets.
- Keep away from flames.
- Wash your hands after handling.

Incorporating Moon Phases and Days of the Week Into Your Spells

One way to give your magickal workings an extra bit of "oomph" is by casting spells during specific times. The moon has a powerful effect on magick, and days of the week are ruled by different planets, meaning you can draw on this celestial energy to add extra power to your spiritual endeavors. While sometimes you may need to work a spell right now, there are other times that you can plan ahead, meaning you can tie your work to specific times to make it that much more powerful.

Moon Phases

The moon has a strong relationship to magick and intuition. It has a remarkable effect on our planet, being responsible for tides, and as it ebbs and flows, so do its effects on our magickal workings. Different moon phases are optimized for different things in the following ways (Raine, 2012):

- **New moon:** New beginnings and "planting seeds," especially for things you would like to bring to fruition during a lunar cycle.
- **Waxing moon:** Attracting things to yourself, such as love and prosperity.
- **Full moon:** The most powerful time for

magick and psychism. A time for celebration—many Wiccans mark the full moon as "esbats"—and important divination and spell work.

- **Waning moon:** Releasing what does not serve you and banishing negativity.

Days of the Week

As well as the moon phase, you can work with the days of the week. Each day is ruled by one of the traditional astrological planets and thus takes on their characteristics. This means that each day is primed to be better than others for casting spells relating to their reigning planet. Roger Horne (2019) explains it well in his book *Folk Witchcraft:*

Sunday is ruled by the sun and is associated with healing, happiness, and good fortune. Monday is ruled by the moon and is associated with the second sight [ability to see spirits] and divination. Tuesday is ruled by Mars and is associated with defense and victory over enemies. Wednesday is ruled by Mercury and is associated with trade, communication, and travel. Thursday is ruled by Jupiter and associated with prosperity, luck, and favor. Friday is ruled by Venus and is associated with love, friendship, and beauty. Finally, Saturday is ruled by Saturn, associated with curses, the dead, and baneful workings. (p.33)

Color Magick

Colors, too, carry power. Just as each color has its

own wavelength scientifically, so each carries its own specific energy corresponding to different magickal intentions. You can thus incorporate colors into your magickal workings according to what you are seeking to gain. Popular ways to do this involve candles or thread, depending on the form of spell you are using. The meanings of each color are as follows (Chamberlain, 2017a; Saint Thomas, 2018; Wiginton, 2018):

- **Red:** Love, passion, lust, courage, defense, conflict, and power.
- **Pink:** Romance, pure/innocent love, friendship, and self-care.
- **Orange:** Creativity, attraction, physical energy, and self-expression.
- **Yellow:** Abundance, self-confidence, communication, academic pursuits, and happiness.
- **Green:** Prosperity, material possessions, money, and fertility.
- **Light blue:** Peace and healing.
- **Dark blue:** Psychic abilities, protection, and empathy.
- **Purple:** Intuition and psychic ability, deity work, ambition, and power.
- **Black:** Protection and banishing.
- **White:** Cleansing, purity, connection to the divine, and the truth.

- **Gray:** Complexity, balance, and binding.
- **Brown:** The earth, material possessions, the home, and animals.
- **Gold:** The sun, money, prosperity, and careers.
- **Silver:** The moon, intuition, and psychism.

Working With Deities, Spirits, and Ancestors for Protection

Another way you can protect yourself is by enlisting the help of the various incorporeal entities that surround us. Spirits (particularly spirit guides), ancestors, and deities can all have relationships developed with them, after which point you can ask them for aid in protection.

Who to choose? Well, it all depends on your personal predilections. With deities in particular, many people feel the need to select the "right" one for the job. However, all deities have it within their magnificent abilities to offer protection by dint of their power. Even a deity associated with the gentle realm of love, Aphrodite, carried the cult epithet (a bit like a surname for gods) *Areia* in Ancient Greece, meaning "warlike" (*Aphrodite Titles*, n.d.).

What is more important than the domains that the gods rule over is your personal relationship with them, and this is true with spirits and ancestors as well. In Ancient Greece, this relationship to the divine was known as *kharis,* which can be translated as "grace" or "thankfulness." It describes the relationship of reciprocity between worshipped and worshipper, in which thanks is given for divine assistance and offerings are made even without the expectation of something in return—although when asking for something in particular, it is also considered "best practice" to accompany it with an offering, too (*Kharis (Χάρις) Our Relationship With the Godss*, 2012; Burkert, 1987).

There is also a belief floating around in popular witchcraft circles that states that you need to be "chosen" by a deity to work with them. To put it bluntly, this is false. While sometimes deities do reach out to practitioners, it is just as valid to be interested in one yourself and initiate the relationship.

So, how do we develop these relationships? It is a similar process for all entities, whether deities, ancestors, or spirit guides, and you needn't possess any of the psychic clair senses in order to be able to do so. Like relationships with other humans, communication is key, as is taking care of their needs. This is quite safe, particularly in the case of most deities and ancestors, despite what some may say in different corners of the internet. After all, in the ancient world, even children would join in celebrations and worship of gods.

With respect to communication, this naturally includes prayer—which looks different to each practitioner—but also divination. You can use any divinatory tool to ask the entity you are contacting to give you answers to questions. This is a great way of checking to see if an offering has been received well, but it can also be used to ask for guidance and advice. This is why most witches devote some time to trying to get accustomed to at least one form of divination because it comes in handy for so many things.

Offerings can take place anywhere, such as in nature, but tend to be made on a shrine dedicated to the entity you are giving them to. Pretty much anything can be an offering, even down to a simple glass of water, so it needn't be pricey at all. Many people will offer the first bite of their meal to entities, too, which you can remove a bitesize portion and place upon the shrine. Other popular offerings include plants sacred to that deity, milk, alcohol, coffee, bread, grains, and honey. Many people will also burn incense in the entities' honor. These perishable offerings can be respectfully disposed of when you feel it is right—many people will "return them to the earth" by burying or leaving them outside—but it is also possible to give gifts that will remain on the shrine permanently, such as crystals, shells, plants, and statues. These are known as "votive offerings" (*Offerings to Gods and Ancestors: Paganism Basics,* 2018; Virginia, 2019; Wigington, 2019a, 2020).

By building a regular practice that involves communication and offerings, you will build up a relationship with your entity of choice. Once this has been done, you can call on them, much like how a friend may call on another friend for a favor. When doing so, be sure to accompany the petition with an offering as a sign of good faith. However, if you need to pray quickly on the fly for assistance, you can mention the good standing relationship you have to persuade the entity for help and provide an offering later when you have the time. You should also typically offer again in thanks once the job is done.

CHAPTER 4
BUILDING YOUR MAGICKAL SHIELD

Your spirit is the true shield. – Morihei Ueshiba

Now that you are more aware of the background of magickal protection as well as the basic constituent parts of magick, we can begin to delve into more detail about how to convert this theory into practice. Let's start with the most basic elements: prayer and building a shield. Both are forms of proactive prevention, meaning they will be there for you before an attack happens. There are many ways you can build shields, in particular, but they typically use the power of visualization and what is called "energy work." I'll explain this in more detail below, as well as ways to cleanse your energy and recoup any that is lost by connecting to the earth and the cosmos. Firstly, however, I'll explain why protecting yourself before attacks is a prudent thing to do.

The Importance of Proactive Prevention

Defending yourself when an attack happens is all well and good, but it immediately places you on the back foot. Chances are you're already beset with symptoms—which is how you know you are being attacked—and you need to act quickly to discern the cause and disarm it.

Surely, then, it makes sense to have something in place before an attack of some kind happens. After all, countries don't stand down their armies in the absence of war: They keep them and continue to train them so that they are both a deterrent to those who would wish a nation harm as well as to ensure they are prepared should someone attempt to attack the country.

Magical defense works in much the same way. We put wards in place and shield ourselves energetically to prevent harm from being done to us. They will disarm attacks before they can take place. While no ward or method of shielding is perfect—meaning there will inevitably be ways around it—they can be powerful at preventing a magickal attack from taking root.

Defending Against Psychic Attacks and Witchcraft: Harnessing Your Inner Power and Intuition for Defense

Now that you know the importance of protecting yourself from magickal attack, you're probably now wondering how you go about doing this. One way is to create wards and protective amulets. These will be the focus of the next chapter. What I want to talk about here, however, is something you can tap into at any point: shielding. This combines grounding, visualization, and directed intention—three of the most important basic skills in witchcraft—to work with your own energy reserves. Because the techniques involved are so fundamental to spell casting, it is worth covering them here, as this will then be built on in subsequent chapters when it comes to casting more advanced (but still beginner-friendly) spells.

Shielding

So, what is shielding? It is exactly what it sounds like: the erection of a magickal shield of energy around yourself that prevents external influences from coming in and interfering. Think of science fiction films and television shows like *Star Trek:* They all talk about shields on spaceships that prevent missiles from landing. They take the damage of these attacks and keep the actual vessel itself from coming to harm. Magickal shields work in much the same way.

The basic way of shielding can be done on the fly, whenever you want negative energy to run off you like water off a duck's back. All you need is a moment or two to devote to putting your shield in place. When you first begin, it may take a little bit longer to be able to do this, but over time, it will become second nature.

The directions to shield are as follows:

1. Bring your attention to your breath. If it helps, place a hand gently on your tummy to feel the inhales and exhales. Take a moment to really concentrate on this. Clear the mind as best as possible. If unwanted thoughts intrude, acknowledge them by saying to yourself, "Thinking," and then, gently redirect attention back onto the breath.

2. Feel the ground under your feet. Feel your weight pressing down upon it, and the solidity that supports you always. Picture, in your mind, deep roots coming from your feet into the ground. The earth is a constant reservoir of energy: Feel yourself drawing this up through your rooted feet. You may picture this as white light, pure and malleable for your intention.

3. Now, picture outer space above you. Celestial energy—whether that's from the moon, the sun, planets, or the stars—has an indelible effect on us. Feel yourself drawing this energy down through the crown of your head.

4. Sit with this combination for a moment, feeling

yourself pulling energy from the earth and the cosmos in tandem. It will land in the center of your body, right behind your solar plexus. This is one method in the practice we call "grounding."

5. Next, when you are ready, "push out" this energy so that it forms a sphere of white light around you. Hold this feeling while thinking your intention clearly: You are protected from magickal attack and negative influence. You may choose to chant something to this effect, such as

> As above, so below,
> I am protected through this flow.
> Shielding me, sheltering me,
> From negative influence, I am free.

6. Once you feel adequately protected, you may cease the visualization, knowing that the shield will remain in place. "Top it up" throughout the day if you feel it is necessary. Over time, you will find it easier to sense this energy by using your intuition pretty much reflexively. However, while you are building this skill, you may wish to pause for a moment to focus on the breath again to then "feel out" what your energy feels like and if the shield is still working optimally.

Prayers For Protection: Drawing on Deities and Your Ancestors

Prayer is one way that we commune with deities and sometimes ancestors by speaking our wishes either aloud or internally to them. Because of this, they can be done at any time, in any place. While it is customary to provide an offering with a prayer, if you are out and about, you can do this step later.

Many people worry about saying the wrong thing when praying, but essentially, all you need to do is speak from the heart. So long as what you are saying corresponds with your intentions and is said in an appropriately respectful way, the exact wording of your prayer does not matter. This means you can do it whenever you want, as opposed to only when you have written materials to hand to refer to.

While many people also enjoy writing their prayers to create something more formal, that nevertheless uses their own wording, there is nothing wrong with using a prayer written by someone else. Below are two prayers that I have personally written: one to Mother Nature—called many things within different religions that recognize the divinity of the earth—and another to our ancestors. Feel free to work these prayers into your own magickal practice.

Prayer to Mother Nature

Mother, mother, she who gives,
Upon your face is all that lives,

Ruler over big and small,
Your magnificence is known by all.
I pray today to your holy self,
To ask for protection and good health.
Shield me please from evil and harm,
And bless my mind with total calm.
Look after me and all that I love,
As below and as above.

Prayer to the Ancestors

Ancestors, hear my humble plea:
I thank you for watching over me.
I ask now for your protection.
From all forms of malediction.
Keep me and my loved ones safe and sound,
And to you, there'll be praise all around.

Strengthening Your Aura and Energy Field

Working with energy in this magickal way can be draining. This is one of the reasons that you pull energy from the earth and celestial bodies when doing any form of energy work, like that involved in shielding, as it will help to stop you from being depleted.

If you do feel tired after magick, you should take time to rest. Eating and drinking are also important and will make you feel much better. Additionally, you can reconnect with the earth through your roots and allow any excess energy that may make you feel jittery to drain into it. This is another form of grounding. Over time, you will get better at manipulating your energy as well as that around you and in your tools, meaning magickal burnout of some variety will be much less likely to happen.

Sometimes, our energy can get muddled, though, and it leaves us feeling out of sorts. We just feel a little funky all over or "off," but we can't put a finger on why. Many ancient religions spoke of "pollution" that we pick up in our day-to-day lives. The Ancient Greeks called this miasma, seeing it as something we collect up through human activities such as getting physically dirty, having been around excesses of emotion, having sex, and also experiencing times such as sickness and death as well as birth. Before the Greeks would pray or enter a temple, they would cleanse themselves with their equivalent of holy water, making themselves pure before the gods (*Purification in Hellenismos*, 2013).

Knowing this about the idea of pollution makes this "off" feeling make sense. We're carrying around energetic baggage from our daily lives, and it lingers about, sapping us of energy and alertness, as well as possibly making any magickal activity less successful because you can't direct a pureness of energy into your spells quite so easily. This is why I used the word "muddled" before because it is kind of like everything is a bit mixed up, and so, you're being pulled in multiple directions at once, rather than being able to focus and live through your intentions.

Cleansing

Fortunately, there are ways to get rid of these negative or polluting influences. Enter cleansing, sometimes called purification: This is the magickal process by which you give something a spiritual deep-clean, getting rid of what you do not need and reviving that which you do. This is something you can do to yourself, your space, and objects—particularly those that are second-hand, as they are more likely to carry traces of other people's energy.

There are many methods you can use to cleanse something. With all of these, you should make sure to cover the entire space, whether that's around your body, the room, the house, or around the object. Do not neglect nooks, crannies, or corners. Some methods of cleansing include the following (Sebastiani, 2018):

- Using incense: This can take the form of a smoke cleansing bundle—often erroneously called "smudge sticks"—censing with herbs burned (safely!) on charcoal, or with stick incense that can be found cheaply in many locations both online and in the flesh. Make sure the smoke actually touches whatever it is cleansing.

- Sprinkling holy water: This is usually prayed over to bless and consecrate it to the task and is typically composed of water with some sea salt added. You may also add cleansing herbs to it.

- Washing and cleaning: When it comes to yourself, this means a salt scrub in the shower infused with cleansing herb essences or a bath filled with some salt and purifying herbs—or a pre-made infusion of these if you don't want to be picking bits of herb out of the tub afterward! For spaces and objects, this means giving everything a clean. You can wash floors, walls, and water-safe knickknacks using an infusion of cleansing herbs and use a broom to sweep up—extra points if it is a traditional witch's besom, which looks exactly like the sort of brooms fairytale witches fly upon.

- Sprinkling a specially made cleansing powder: This is made up of pulverized herbs corresponding to these cleansing intentions. Sprinkle them all over, and then, sweep or vacuum it up before emptying the contents outside of the property; after all, if you're trying to rid yourself of something, you don't want it sticking around in the bin!

- Using sound: You may ring a bell, chant, or stomp your feet and clap your hands. When doing the latter, you may also shout out commands for the energy to leave. This more noisy method is particularly effective as the stage you would take before banishing a spirit and after asking it to leave politely.

- The use of fire and light: This would mean

safely carrying a candle around and shining its light upon every part of the thing you wish to cleanse.

Many people work cleansing into a schedule of sorts, using the beginnings-related energy of the new moon to cleanse and purify their spaces, and it is also common to cleanse the self before any ritual, offerings, or spell work. On top of this, many witches also habitually revive their wards at certain times, too. These wards are the subject of the next chapter.

CHAPTER 5

THE FIRST LINE OF DEFENSE: PROTECTION MAGICK

Self-defense is not just a set of techniques, it's a state of mind that begins with the belief that you are worth defending. — Rorion Gracie

You've now been equipped with some of the basics of witchcraft, as well as the knowledge of protective herbs and crystals. You've also been able to begin practicing magick through the construction of a shield and methods of cleansing. This is a good foundation for what comes next: proactive protection magick. In this chapter, I'll walk you through how to come up with what sort of protection you'd like to construct, before giving you some ready-made spells that you can cast whenever the fancy takes you. However, at the end of the chapter, I'll cover how to write your own spells, meaning you can also take those listed here as inspiration and alter them to better fit your purposes—as well as what materials you have at hand. This chapter, then, will serve as a strong foundational practice of witchcraft aimed at protecting you from magickal or psychic attack.

Creating a Personal Protection Plan

I have previously spoken about layering up your protections. Rather than scattering your energy in one spell that attempts to do too many things at once—in which the blowback is harder to predict because of the vagueness of the intentions—it is better to put some time into multiple, more targeted spells. While this requires some planning, the energy used shouldn't differ too much from one big, far-reaching spell that would require massive amounts to actually achieve its aims.

So, what sort of spells should you do? That all depends on what you want to protect. As a minimum, I would recommend warding yourself and your property against harm. You may break this down further into wards specifically targeting certain things, such as protection from spirits and protection from theft. This means you can tinker and tailor your approach to all your different needs. You can also use what you learned in the previous chapter about shielding and cleansing to combine with wards and create a comprehensive plan of protection.

Magick, however, will never last forever. It requires energy and to be refreshed. Many witches use the lunar cycle as a marker of when they cleanse and ward, such as every new moon. This doesn't necessarily look like starting from scratch, depending on what methods you have chosen, but may look like "feeding" energy to your already existing wards by completely burning an enchanted candle in their presence.

When it comes to planning when to cleanse and shield yourself, you will need to factor in your own circumstances. Someone who works in a customer-facing role will be more likely to need to do this more often than someone who works from home. Natural empaths—which you'll remember are people who can feel the emotions of others without being told about them—also tend to need to do this more regularly, as I have already stated.

It is worth, then, thinking about your own circumstances before deciding what your personal protection plan should look like. Research the different types of spells—using those contained within this book as inspiration—to see what will work best for you. For instance, if you need to be discreet about your craft, a jar spell or another physically enchanted object probably isn't the best choice.

Once you have an idea of what will work for you, write it down somewhere you won't forget it. Many witches advise the keeping of a grimoire or "book of shadows": a specially crafted journal or document that you populate with all things related to your craft, such as research, experiment notes, and spell logs. If you haven't already started one of these, I would strongly recommend it, as recordkeeping allows you to track your practice as a witch over time. A personal protection plan would fit into this sort of book.

Protective Circles and Barriers

Many witches and other practitioners of magick will "cast a circle" before carrying out magick and rituals. But what is this? Essentially, a circle is a demarcation of spiritual space that both holds energy within it to power a spell while also keeping out unwanted interference (Wigington, 2018b). In a way, it's a bit like the shields we have already discussed, except this time it's about protecting a space. While not every witchcraft practice requires a circle, and sometimes, you need to do a spell on the fly without time to prepare something like this, casting a circle does carry the benefits I have already mentioned, as well as helping you to get into the right frame of mind for magick through the ritual actions. As such, I would recommend casting one when you do have the opportunity to prepare your magickal workings.

Casting a circle is fortunately a very beginner-friendly practice. Each witch will have a different method of doing so, some more elaborate than others, and some that call on the guardians of the elements.

Here is mine, which you'll find is quite simple. To cast this circle, you will need a wand or athame. In a pinch, you can use the index finger on your dominant, projecting hand.

The directions are as follows (Alexander, 2014):

1. Have your workspace all ready to go, making sure you have all the tools and ingredients necessary to complete your spell.
2. Ground and center yourself using the methods already outlined in this book, pulling energy from the earth and the celestial sphere.
3. Holding your wand or athame, or pointing out your finger if you do not have these, face west. Visualizing your energy pouring forth from your finger, slowly turn clockwise and see it drawing a sphere all the way around you, until you face the same direction again.

If at any point you need to leave the circle, use the wand, athame, or your finger to cut a doorway out of it, making sure to close it behind you. When you return, you will need to do the same thing again.

Dismantling a circle after your spell work or ritual is done involves the same steps as casting one, except instead of turning clockwise (sometimes known as "deosil"), you turn counter-clockwise (sometimes known as "widdershins") and imagine the energy falling away. This is because moving clockwise in magic is used to invoke, while counter-clockwise is for banishment.

Evoking Deities, Guardian Spirits, and Guides for Protection

There is some confusion in the witchcraft community about the difference between "invoking" and "evoking" gods, spirits, ancestors, and guides. Often, these terms are erroneously used interchangeably. However, there is a difference between these. To invoke an entity is to offer oneself up as a vessel for their power so that they appear in this realm through you. As such, it is more akin to a form of consensual possession. Evoking, on the other hand, is an invitation for the entity to join your ritual or spell work, usually to lend their power to you in an external way (Wigington, 2017).

So, how do you go about evoking a deity or guide of sorts for protection while conducting magick or to protect you in general? In fact, I have already covered this in Chapter 3. Evoking involves the same sort of communication that you would usually use for entities. To evoke one is to ask them to attend a ritual and lend their power to it whilst providing them with an offering for them to do so. This would be done after you have created your magickal circle but before you commence the spell work itself.

Once done, you will likely feel a shift in the energy of the circle, if this is something you are attuned to, or perhaps a sensation in your body of something else being there. If you can't feel anything, don't worry: Perceiving energetic changes around you and the presence of entities is a form of psychism, and it develops as a skill over time.

Once you have finished your spell work, you would thank whoever you have evoked for attending before you dismantle your circle. You may then make an offering later, at the time the spell has had its desired effect.

As said in Chapter 3, entities such as deities, ancestors, and spirit guides can also be evoked on the fly if you feel you need protection. Simply say a prayer—either out loud or in your head—asking for help, potentially referencing how good your relationship with the entity is, and then make an offering later when you have the ability to do so.

Warding Your Home, Workplace, and Personal Space

Now that I have covered how to prepare a sacred space for your spell work that will also help to raise and contain energy while keeping out external influence you'd rather not engage with, we can come to the exciting bit: "proper" spells!

Below are a selection of protection spells from my personal grimoire. These are aimed at creating wards for your property. We'll start with sigils because these are a magickal technique that can be applied in a variety of ways to create powerful spells that require less effort and fewer ingredients. I'll then go through some spells that can be used for your house and your car—two pieces of property that people like to enchant with a protective energy. These spells, however, can be adapted to be used for other items of value to yourself; at the end of this chapter, I'll go through how to write your own spells, which will allow you to alter anything I have written for different purposes.

Making Sigils for Multiple Uses

Sigil comes from the Latin *"sigillum"* meaning "seal," but in occult spaces, it refers to a symbol created for magickal purposes (Merriam-Webster, n.d.-b). In this sense, we can say that we take our energy and intent and seal it into a magickal device of sorts that allows us to utilize that power whenever we draw the sigil onto something.

Originally taken as a concept from ceremonial magick, the modern-day usage of sigils comes from the work of chaos magicians, such as Peter J Carrol (Woodfield, 2022). However, one needn't follow this particular tradition to practice sigil magick. Popularity has exploded in recent years for this method, and you can see why: By magickally forging a symbol that carries such power, we can use it as and when required to quickly cast a spell. This is an incredibly handy technique to have in your repertoire!

So, how do you make a sigil? Kerry Woodfield (2022) gives a comprehensive overview of the various techniques to do this in her book *Sigil Magick,* but I will condense the steps here and combine them with my own personal method of making a sigil. The steps are as follows, and you will need a pen, paper, a cauldron (or other heatproof dish), and either a lighter or matches:

1. Prepare your sacred space, as well as yourself, by grounding and centering your mind on the task at hand. This may involve some level of meditation and breathwork to activate a more magickal state of mind.

2. Think about how to word your intent as concisely as possible but only in terms of positives. Don't use negative words. So, instead of saying, "Do not let harm come to me," you would say, "Protect me."

3. Write out your intent on a piece of paper. Cross out all the vowels and any repeating letters. This is the first level of abstraction, as sigil magick is dependent on the end result not being legible as a word or phrase.

4. Now is the fun part! Play with the shapes of the remaining letters to create a design. It needn't be ornate or a piece of award-winning art: So long as there is a level of abstraction between the symbol and what it is supposed to represent, it will work.

5. Next, it is time to charge your sigil. Place your dominant hand on top of the completed

mark—this is the hand that projects energy. Now, ground yourself as you have already learned, pulling energy from the earth and the celestial realm. Focus your mind entirely on your intent. Visualize, in detail, using all the senses if possible, what that intent looks like when it is enacted.

6. Once the energy has built to a point that you can no longer hold anymore, see it flowing from you into the sigil. You will know when you have emptied the energy into it.

7. Make a copy of the sigil if you intend to use it regularly so that you will not forget it. Your grimoire/book of shadows would work well as a reliquary for these.

8. Fold the piece of paper that you have charged towards you—this is how to invoke; folding away from the body is used to banish). Light it on fire, and then place it in a heatproof dish to burn out completely. Sprinkle the ashes onto the earth outside or into a plant pot if you do not have access to a green space.

There is debate about whether or not one should look at a sigil after it has been made. Some say it should be forgotten consciously so that the subconscious mind can power it. Others say this does not matter at all and like to reuse sigils. I am of the latter camp, personally. So long as the sigil has been charged and released into the world upon its creation, it can be harnessed with further intent and energy to be used multiple times. Indeed, it is worth me giving some examples of places where you may put a sigil of protection:

- drawn onto the bottom of your shoe
- sewn into the inside lining of a coat or jacket
- on a piece of paper folded up and placed in your purse or wallet
- drawn using consecrated water—salt water prayed over to bless it with the holiness of the self or of a deity—onto walls, windows, or doors
- drawn onto the inside of a car's glove box
- doodled onto the arm
- drawn on the face when applying makeup and then blended out for subtlety
- drawn on the self using moisturizer and then rubbed into the body
- stirred into your morning coffee or other hot drink to be ingested
- traced in the air using incense

As you can see, there are some temporary and some permanent methods of using a sigil here. Naturally, those that are temporary will need to be recharged with intent and energy more regularly as it is always good to refresh your wards. However, just because it is drawn and then disappears does not diminish the strength of the sigil. One of the benefits of this method is that it can be used in so many ways. I'm sure that, with practice, you will come up with some of your own.

Jar Spell for Home Protection

Jar spells are all over social media at the moment and draw on the long tradition of the witch bottles that I covered in Chapter 1. This particular jar spell is designed to protect your home from being invaded by negativity in any form and send the negative energy back to where it came from. If you would prefer it to simply protect, rather than bite back, you can remove the nails. Do also ensure that the herbs you use are dried: Any moisture content will cause the jar to grow mold. If it still grows mold, you can then know that it has likely caught harm coming towards the home, and therefore, the ward needs to be replaced.

Time

Perform this during the waxing moon on a Tuesday to draw on the power of bringing protection towards you.

Ingredients

- A red candle and something to inscribe it, such as your athame
- A protective incense such as frankincense
- A small glass jar
- Seven nails, preferably iron (iron is associated with protection, and the number seven is particularly magickal)

- Salt (associated with nullifying magick and cleansing)
- Vervain
- Chamomile
- Basil
- Garlic
- Rosemary
- A piece of obsidian that can fit into the jar
- A piece of red jasper that can also fit in the jar

Directions

1. Prepare for the spell work in the usual way.
2. Light the incense.
3. Inscribe the candle with a protective sigil or simply the word "protection" before lighting it.
4. Pass the glass jar through the incense smoke saying

   With the smoke, I cleanse and charge,

   By my will, you will protect this home.
5. Begin to fill the jar. With each ingredient, pour your personal energy and intention into it. Each time, pass the items through the incense smoke as you instruct them of their role. Any words will do, but make sure they relate to the item's correspondences and purpose. For instance, with the basil, say you are drawing on it to protect the home, whereas with the nails, you would say they both protect and return the harm back to whence it came.

6. Once the jar is filled, seal it with the candle wax.

Warding Powder

As I showed in the last chapter, powders can be useful for cleansing. However, they can also be used for warding. This powder is constructed in advance to be used not just immediately but in the future, too. This means it is easy to refresh, as you will simply need to re-sprinkle it.

Time

Make this during the waning moon on a Tuesday to draw on the power of banishing harm. Sprinkle it at regular intervals, such as on the first Tuesday of each waning moon.

Ingredients

- Rosemary
- Nettle
- Onion powder
- Garlic powder
- Pepper
- Bay leaf

Make sure to really grind up the ingredients by using a mortar and pestle so that the warding powder is as fine as you can make it. As you do so, instruct it on its role, perhaps chanting the words "protect and banish." Use the energy generated by the grinding motion to charge the powder.

Once made, this can then be sprinkled around the perimeter of your property. However, if you cannot encircle your property, sprinkling it around the entrances to your home will suffice.

Protection Charm for the Car

Many people worry about their cars and journeys within them and so choose to create a special protection charm for them. This spell works in the same way as the jar spell: through depositing the enchanted ingredients, first passed through incense, into the bag. This spell, however, has two differences: Firstly, you needn't use a candle as you won't be sealing the bag in this way. Secondly, you will knot the bag three times to close it up once the spell is done because the number three is another witchy, magickal number. Once created, you can either hang the pouch from your rear mirror or store it away in your glove box for something more subtle.

Time

Create these protection charms on a Wednesday, which is associated with travel, and during a waxing moon.

Ingredients
- A small red pouch
- A small piece of lapis lazuli
- A small piece of tiger's eye
- A cinnamon stick
- A bay leaf

Amulets for Protection of the Self

Now that I have covered how to ward property, I can move on to my spell that revolves around protecting the self. When it comes to this, it can be better to have something that relates to you specifically because it carries your energy. This is why this particular spell uses a piece of jewelry that you already have. Because it is meaningful to you, it has a strong tie that can be manipulated by magick to protect you. The spell itself can be adapted with ease for a variety of circumstances: general protection, protection from the evil eye—using a nazar here would be doubly useful— or protection during travel. This spell, then, takes an everyday object and consecrates it to be worn daily.

Time

Imbue your amulet with magick on a Tuesday during the waxing moon.

Ingredients

- A bowl (perhaps your cauldron) of salt water
- Your chosen piece of jewelry
- Protective incense such as frankincense
- A red candle and your athame to inscribe it with

Directions

1. Prepare for the spell as you usually would.
2. Light the incense.
3. Inscribe the candle with a protective sigil or the word "protection," and light it.

4. Pass the jewelry through the smoke of the incense, saying, "By power of air, I enchant you to protect."

5. Pass the jewelry over the flame of the candle (without touching it), saying, "By power of flame, I enchant you to protect."

6. Sprinkle the jewelry with the salt water, saying, "By power of earth and water, I enchant you to protect."

7. Hold the jewelry in your hands, and fill it with your own energy and intent, clearly visualizing in positive terms what you would like it to do.

8. Conclude the spell as you usually would.

Designing Your Own Protection Spells and Charms

The amount of spells that you can do for protection is limited only by your imagination and access to resources. The latter will accumulate over time as you build up the physical arsenal of your magickal workings, and you needn't rush out to buy everything straight away, as I have already said.

The former, however, can be difficult to tap into, especially when you're first starting out with magick. There is a way you can build your imagination, however: building your knowledge. Witchcraft isn't always the glamorous casting of spells, you see. It involves dedication, and some of that needs to be around educating yourself about magick. The fact that you've picked up this book and gotten this far is a sign that you're committed. However, one source is never enough. I encourage you to go out and research any of the concepts in this book further; the references section at the end will be able to direct you to the sources I have drawn from throughout. By educating yourself in this way, you will be able to start building your own spells.

So, what does the spell-writing process look like? You might break it down into stages as follows:

1. **Decide what the spell is for**: This would mean thinking about your intent and what you want to achieve. It is best to be as specific here as possible so that your energy is not scattered.

2. **Decide the method of the spell:** Do you want to make a jar or sachet? How about an amulet? Or perhaps, you need a quick candle spell for a one-off event you're trying to bring about or prevent? Consider your intention and what form of spell would best suit it.

3. **Choose your ingredients**: Refer to correspondence lists to find ingredients that match your intention. You might also look into the folklore surrounding certain objects, the psychology of color, or even the medicinal qualities of certain herbs. If you're trying to cast a spell that helps with nightmares, for instance, a herb that assuages anxiety and aids sleep, such as valerian, may come in useful.

4. **Choose your timing:** Refer to the moon

phases and days of the week in Chapter 3, and choose the best time for your spell. This will give it an added celestial boost.

5. **Plan the steps:** Once you know everything you need to complete the spell, the method you're using, and why you're actually doing it, you can begin to plot out the steps. It is best practice to write these steps down to refer back to later, and so, they should be put in your grimoire or book of shadows. Make sure that your explanation is easy to follow and every step makes sense. Consider writing your own spoken words to accompany certain actions, for words have power and help us to focus our intent and energy on the spell. They needn't rhyme, although sometimes it feels more magickal for them to do so.

Once you have completed the spell, make a dated record of how it went and if you made any changes while actually doing it. Later, record the outcome of the spell: Did it work? How? Were there any unforeseen consequences? By keeping records of your magickal workings, you can chart your progress over time.

Ideas That You Can Build a Spell Around

It would be remiss of me to leave you here without a little more guidance. Instead of fleshing out more spells for you, I want to give you the opportunity to come up with your own based on some prompts.

These little kernels of magick can be taken and have a more formal spell written around them—one as complicated or simple as you wish it to be.

These ideas come from folk magick and knowledge or correspondences. You will develop quite the collection of nuggets of information about these things as you progress in your research into witchcraft. For now, however, here are those that I have picked out for you to experiment with (King, 2016; Pennick, 2021):

- Tie a naturally "holey stone" to your keys to guard your home; holey stones are pebbles with naturally occurring holes, and they are thought to be protective.
- Hang a horseshoe above your front door—upwards to attract luck or downwards to protect from evil.
- Draw sigils on the bottoms of your shoes to protect you when you go out walking.
- Plant a protective herb either outdoors or in a pot for indoor display (checking which is appropriate for your chosen flora), and tend to it, giving it instructions to protect the home.
- Create a poppet (usually incorrectly called "voodoo dolls") to represent someone, and fill it with protective herbs and crystals.
- Make a witch's ladder—a string with feathers and other charms tied onto it at intervals—to

be hung in the home for protection.

- Create a wash for the home out of herbs or essential oils (remembering the safety tips from Chapter 3) to wash down windows and doors with.

- Craft an enchanted oil that can be used to anoint people and objects.

- Using your favorite method of art, create something that you pour your creative energy into to use as a ward, such as a painting, a clay ornament, or a knitted blanket—great for protecting children from nightmares.

Anoint a candle, carve a sigil upon it, and allow it to burn down completely.

CHAPTER 6
REACTIVE MAGICK

Remember, your words can plant gardens or burn whole forests down. – Gemma Troy

With proactive protection in place, you're covered from a wide variety of harms. However, sometimes, things still slip through the net and catch us unawares. That's why it pays to know how to perform reactive magick before you need to do it because, then, you're prepared for any eventuality.

What do I mean by reactive magick? This is essentially any spell that is used in reaction to harm and includes things like hex-breaking and banishing. You may also wish to give a bit of a kick up the butt to the person sending negative energy your way. In this case, you will likely be interested in a return-to-sender spell.

It's not up to me to tell you the rights or wrongs of this action: Your ethics are your own business, and as we covered in Chapter 1, different people will view these things differently. However, it would be remiss of me to not include this in case you are of a mind that you would like to do a spell such as this.

Therefore, this chapter is a compendium of tactics on how to respond to magickal or psychic harm. Follow on as I walk you through how to deal with hexes and how to banish negative influences in your space.

Uncrossing and Hex-Breaking Spells

You may come across a variety of terms to describe spells that remove curses and hexes as well as psychic attacks. In this section, I will go through what an "uncrossing" spell is while paying attention to the difficult issue that is cultural appropriation, something that I covered briefly in the introduction when talking about traditions involving initiation. I will then give you a template spell for hex-breaking. While this spell will work on its own if followed correctly, you can also adapt it for your own uses, potentially making it more specific to your needs or substituting ingredients you do not have by using the correspondence list in Chapter 3. This section, then, will go through all you need to know about how to remove curses in a way that does not send them back to wherever they came from, as that is the focus of the section that follows.

Uncrossing Spells and Cultural Appropriation

In a thesis written by Kathryn Gottlieb (2017), a definition of cultural appropriation is given:

Cultural appropriation suggests a number of things: that the person doing the appropriating is in some way more powerful than the group they are appropriating from (for example, a white person who is inherently privileged in most of Western society); that the appropriation is done without the consent of the group that is being appropriated from (if an individual is given a piece of cultural material as a gift, it is not generally seen as cultural appropriation); and that the appropriation in some way does harm to the group that is being appropriated from (for example, if the appropriation perpetuates stereotypes). (p. 4)

It is also often defined as one group benefitting from another. For example, if someone manages to make money off of a culture that is not their own, they are appropriating. The same can be said of gaining social acclaim for one's appropriation, particularly when people from the culture in question often receive negativity for taking part in their heritage.

How does this apply to uncrossing spells? A quick Google search shows many oils used for such magick for sale. On one website, however, it is pointed out that such spells come from African diasporic practices such as Hoodoo (*Uncrossing: Removing Negative Energy* 2021).

As I have already covered, these practices are considered closed to outsiders. This is because of a complex interplay of factors. Hoodoo and other such diasporic practices come from the spirituality of enslaved peoples who tried to keep alive the spirit of the religions they followed on their home continent while adapting to a life of Christianity. As such, they are syncretic between these religions and, most importantly, carry a history of persecution as well as being a constant reminder of the oppression of Black people during this period. Because of this, it is mostly agreed upon that only people of African descent can practice these religions and spiritualities, whether or not this is an initiatory tradition like Haitian Vodou or something more akin to folk magick like Hoodoo.

Because of this, and the fact that I am not Black, I will not be taking it upon myself to share an uncrossing ritual, as it goes against my personal values of respecting the cultural traditions of other people in the ways that they have requested. If you are desperate to know more, there are a plethora of resources about this online. However, as with all ethical issues within witchcraft—of which there are many, as you have seen—I encourage you to think carefully about whether or not it is appropriate for you to take this type of spell work into your own spiritual practice.

A Method for Hex-Breaking

There are, nevertheless, many ways you can break a hex, and fortunately, they are accessible for those unfamiliar with such magick. You already know of one: The egg cleanse and divination covered in Chapter 2 can work to remove curses if they are present. In this case, you would cleanse until the yolk is no longer showing signs of a curse being present (such as breaking).

However, if you're looking for something else to do, there is one spell I have created that uses a poppet, which as I have already said is often erroneously called a "voodoo doll." While poppets are used by some rootworkers, they also appear in many folk magick practices across the globe and are therefore an open method that we can use to divert the curse or hex and then eventually break it entirely.

Time
If it is possible to wait, hex-breaking will be most effective on the night of the new moon.
Ingredients
- Black cotton, thread, and a needle to sew
- A taglock associated with you, such as hair or nail clippings
- Frankincense incense
- Thistle
- A bay leaf
- A black pen
- Chili
- Nettle

- Vervain

Directions

1. Prepare for the ritual in your usual way.
2. Light the incense.
3. Begin to construct a basic poppet. Cut two pieces out of the cotton in a shape that resembles a human. Sew mostly together, leaving a gap through which you can stuff it.
4. Pass all the herbs apart from the bay leaf through incense while instructing them of their purpose to break the hex placed against you, and stuff these herbs inside the poppet.
5. Write the words "free from curses" on the bay leaf, pass it through the incense smoke, and place it inside the poppet.
6. Pass the taglock through the incense smoke, and place it inside the poppet, saying

   With part of me, you become my copy,
   Do this job, and don't be sloppy!
   In my place, you take this curse,
   Back to my usual state I will reverse.
   Across this moon, you work for me,
   At the next new moon, I shall be free.
7. Sew up the poppet.
8. Hold the poppet in your hands, and say

   With my breath, I give you life,
   You will free me from this strife.
9. Breathe across the poppet. It is now activated, so to speak. You can now place it away

somewhere hidden but which you will nevertheless not forget.

10. At the next new moon, dispose of the poppet somewhere away from your property. If you can, bury it beneath the earth, but otherwise, ensure you get rid of it entirely.

Return-to-Sender Spells

Sometimes, we don't want to play nice. Sometimes, someone or something will only be deterred from harming you if you bite back. Maybe, you're just royally peeved by their behavior and think they need to learn a lesson. In these instances, you may decide to opt for a return-to-sender spell. As well as breaking a curse or magickal attack, these spells will also turn the harm caused back onto whoever is sending it your way. It is a cost-effective (in terms of energy expended) way of both nullifying an attack against you and hexing someone in return: Instead of doing two separate spells, you can do just one and it will be done.

Spiky Shields

Also relevant to this section is the notion of adapting the shields you learned to construct in Chapter 4 to also redirect negative energy back to where it came from. I'll cover this first as it is the most simple of the techniques covered here. I call these protections "spiky shields" partly because of the visualization of them but also because they remind me of a cactus. Cacti protect themselves from predators by growing spikes that will prick and hurt those who attempt to harm them. Spiky shields work in much the same way: They will prick back at any negativity that comes towards you.

The process of creating a spiky shield is quite simple. You would begin the visualization exercise to construct a shield that was covered in Chapter 4. However, when it comes to holding a picture of the shield in your head, you would see spikes sticking out of it. Perhaps, this looks like a cactus, if we use my previous examples, or like thorny vines writhing around the shield. Imagine negative energy coming towards the shield, getting caught on a spike, and retreating in pain.

Hold this visualization in your head until you feel that the shield has formed around you. At this point, it is done, and it can be refreshed in the same ways discussed in Chapter 4.

A Basic Return-to-Sender Spell Template

Let's get back into the more fun stuff, shall we? Below is a return-to-sender spell from my personal grimoire. By allowing a cord between two candles to burn, you will cut the energetic cord of the curse between yourself and the person involved, while the particular ingredients within the spell will ensure that they feel the spell bounce back onto them. It is important that the candles burn down fully, so select small ones that can be burned in one sitting. There are many small, thin spell candles available to purchase online.

Time

Return-to-sender spells are best cast on a Saturday during the waning moon.

Ingredients

- A small black candle that can be burned in one sitting
- A small red candle that can be burned in one sitting
- Your athame for carving the candles
- Red thread
- A heatproof tray or dish large enough to place both candles in with space between them
- Sea salt
- Chili flakes
- Black pepper
- Cactus spikes, rose thorns, or any other sharp materials from plants
- Nettle

Directions

1. Prepare for the spell in the usual way.
2. Carve the black candle with a sigil of your target's name or, if unknown, something you feel represents them.
3. Carve the red candle with a protective sigil.
4. Melt the bottom of the candles with a lighter, enough to soften a little bit of wax, and use this

to stick the candles to the surface of your tray or dish.

5. Circle the candles with sea salt, the herbs, and the spikes or thorns you have selected, pouring your intention into each ingredient and instructing them of their purpose as you do so.

6. Wrap the red thread around the candles seven times to bind them together, securing with three knots.

7. Light the candles and say
You've done me harm, and now, it's your turn,
With these candles, our connection I burn,
Once they are gone, it will be returned to you,
And after that, our business is through.

8. Allow the candles to burn down, including allowing the thread to separate with the flames.

9. Once the spell is done, dispose of the remnants outside away from your property.

10. Cleanse yourself in an appropriate way once the spell has been fully completed—good practice for any baneful magick.

Unraveling Generational Curses

Let me preface this section by saying that generational curses are very rare. As Avery Hart (2023) says, you'll usually know that you're affected by one because they become part of your family's lore. If you're not sure that a generational curse is to blame for your hardship, do some thorough divination before proceeding as usually what is mistaken for a curse is just bad luck or familial cycles of traumatic norms. Consider even procuring the services of a trusted professional diviner for further information.

Essentially, generational curses are long-standing baneful magick cast upon a family, which are then passed down until someone deals with them. Unfortunately, sometimes that person has to be you as, for whatever, reason your ancestors were unable to do so.

However, your ancestors will be your greatest allies in finally dismantling such baneful magick. They will, by dint of being related to you, be interested in seeing these curses gone. Ancestors are there to guide and protect their descendants, after all, and they have the power to do remarkable things in their new life in death. Remember this for the moment, while I take an aside to discuss what generational curses more often are.

Essentially, it is rare for magick to last beyond a generation. It will usually die when the person who cast it dies. But with generational curses, knowledge of it is passed down between members of the family. Everyone knows about it, no matter how long ago it was, and over time, the curse becomes mythologized but still fervently believed in. As belief is so powerful in magick—indeed, it is often said that the best way to curse someone is to make them think you've cursed them and let their subconscious do all the hard work for you—it becomes a self-perpetuating cycle in which the belief ends up being the fuel for the effects. As such, to break the curse, you need to break the belief. This means performing one hell of a hex-breaking spell, drawing on as much theatrics as possible to thoroughly dismantle belief in the curse because the family members believe in the hex-breaker more than the curse that predated it.

So, essentially, breaking a generational curse is about breaking the belief in it. It's more about psychology than anything else. Write down all your beliefs about the curse on one piece of paper and thoroughly interrogate them. Did your relationship end because of the curse, or did things just turn sour when your partner had a wandering eye—something that happens in 15–20% of marriages (Montemayor, 2023)? Then, you need to work on your psychology over a period of time to believe the rational reasons rather than the mystical ones. Remember the golden rule of witchcraft: Mundane explanations are much more unlikely than magickal ones.

However, if you're still not reassured—and perhaps, your family isn't either—it doesn't hurt to do a curse-breaking ritual. The method for hex-breaking already covered will be of use here, and you may adapt it for your specific circumstances. As I have said, your ancestors will want to help; they take a strong interest in their family line and love to act as guides and guardians, and so, calling upon their aid with the spell will be sure to boost its power.

Still struggling? Here is a spell that may help draw on the power of your ancestors. Make sure to again choose a candle small enough to burn in one sitting.

Time

It is most effective to evoke your ancestors on a Tuesday during the waning moon.

Ingredients

- A red candle
- Your athame for carving
- A cauldron with sand in it, for safe burning
- A small stick or twig of oak, ash, or cedar and a marker to write on it
- Olive oil
- Salt water
- Protective incense such as frankincense
- An offering for your ancestors, such as coffee or alcohol (if they drank)

Directions

1. Cast your circle as you usually would.
2. Place the offering upon your workspace, hold your arms into the air spread apart with your hands open, and say

   Ancestors of mine, hear my plea:
   Tonight, I move to set us free.
   With this offering, I call upon you
   To help me see this magick through.

Stand by my side, and lend your aid,
And I shall undo what was once made.

3. Light the protective incense. Cleanse yourself and your ingredients with it, instructing them of their purpose.

4. Anoint the candle with olive oil by rubbing it from bottom to top (avoiding the wick), moving your fingers away from your body—moving away is to banish, while towards is to attract.

5. Carve a sigil on the candle that represents the word "release" to you or, failing that, simply carve that word.

6. Watch the candle as it burns down. Think about all the misfortune of you and your loved ones vanishing and the prosperity and joy that will follow.

7. When the candle is almost entirely burned, grab the stick and write on it "Curse on [your family name]." Hold it in your right hand and say

    Honored tree, you now serve as a representation,
    With my breath, I make this mutation:
    You become the curse, and the curse becomes you.

8. Breathe onto the stick. Snap it in half. Burn both pieces.

9. Once the candle has burned down, dispose of the remnants away from your property—preferably at a crossroads—and scatter the ashes of the stick into the wind away from you.

Turn, walk away, and do not look back.

10. Thoroughly cleanse yourself and the space in which you cast the spell. It is done.

When Cleanses Don't Work: The Basics of Banishing

It is rare to have spiritual visitors who are troublesome in some way. While popular ghost-hunting shows would have you believe that poltergeists and demons are always around the corner, ready to torment humanity, in actual fact, this kind of activity is pretty rare. Most spirits and other nonhuman entities are happy to live and let live and will only really interact with you if you try to work with them—something some witches do, calling it "spirit work."

However, on rare occasions, someone does come and cause ructions. In these circumstances, you should first try to get them to disappear politely. As I have said in previous chapters, you wouldn't immediately start screaming and shouting obscenities at cold callers at your door—or, at least, I hope not! Instead, you can connect with the spirit through divination to find out what they want and see if there's any way you can help them so long as they promise to leave. Otherwise, you can open a window and politely ask them to leave through it. Give your house a thorough cleanse—my favorite method is with smoke cleansing sticks made from cleansing herbs such as rosemary or garden sage—however, not white sage as it is actually endangered and a closed practice to Native Americans.

With these methods, your problem will likely be solved.

Still not budging? Up the ante. Cleanse the house again, and use some sound this time too. Stomp your feet, shout at the entity to leave, and warn it that you will take further action should it not heed your words. Remember the essence of the Terry Pratchett quote at the beginning of this book: Witches should remember that they are feared just as much as unwanted spirits, and you do have the skills to remove them. Back up your words with confidence and strong conviction, and your unwanted lodger will probably clear out.

However, in the rarest of circumstances, the presence may remain. In these instances, when cleansing and telling the entity off does not work, you'll need to take action to forcibly banish them. Some witches frown down upon banishing as a form of baneful magick: After all, you are evicting someone with a bit of a kick up the butt. However, you can't live your life if you have someone meddlesome around who is causing trouble and won't go no matter how firmly you state your desires. As such, it is my opinion that allowing the spirit or entity to remain is causing more harm, as you are hurting yourself! Because of this, I see little to no ethical quandaries when it comes to banishing. So long as you don't jump the gun and banish anything and everything—something which would also end up depleting your energy—you should be fine.

An All-Purpose Banishing Ritual

Below is my purpose-built banishing spell, inspired by Thalia Thorne (2020) but with some changes to personalize it to my style. This spell involves creating your own incense cones, which sounds tricky but is actually rather simple. By creating your own incense, you can pour your intentions into the cones so that when they burn, they release your intentions into your space and pack more of a punch than pre-bought cleansing sticks. The ingredients involved are also specific to banishing as well as the addition of a cleansing herb. The use of a crystal allows you to trap the spirit's link to your space and remove it from the property. It's a bit like physically picking them up and hauling them out the door before locking it behind you.

Time

If possible a Tuesday during the waning moon is best, but usually, banishings cannot wait, and you should not put up with annoyance or harm just because you're waiting for the right moon phase.

Ingredients

- A piece of obsidian
- Salt water
- A red candle
- Your athame for carving
- Distilled water
- Basil
- Frankincense

- Lavender
- Rosemary
- A mortar and pestle

Directions

1. Prepare your space and circle as you usually would. Call on any deities, guides, or ancestors you would like the aid of with an offering.

2. Grind up the herbs in the mortar and pestle while visualizing your intent. Use your rage to power them, telling them what they will do for you.

3. Once the herbs are a fine powder, add a little distilled water to them until they make a paste.

4. Shape the doughy herbs into a cone. Allow it to dry.

5. Once the incense is dried, carve a banishing sigil on the candle. Light it along with your handmade cone.

6. Consecrate the obsidian by passing it through the smoke of the incense, above the flame of the candle, and sprinkling it with salt water, saying something along the lines of
With the power of [air/fire/earth and water], I consecrate this stone
It is now that I make my intention known:
This spirit will be driven away from here,
And then, my environment will be clear.

7. As the candle and incense burn down—which you should allow them to do completely—hold

the crystal in your dominant hand and meditate upon it. Keep your visualization of your intent strong, and feel the energy of the spirit and its connection to you and your space pouring into the obsidian.

8. Once the candle and incense are completely burned, take the spell's ingredients, along with the crystal, to an open space away from your home. Dispose of all the ingredients except the stone, preferably by burying them in the earth.

9. Hold the stone in your dominant hand and say
   Spirit, you are trapped, and my
   [gods/ancestors/guides] have been called upon,
   By our will, you will be gone!

10. Throw the stone as far away from you as possible. Turn around, walk away, and don't look back. The spirit will trouble you no more.

11. Once you have returned home, thoroughly cleanse the house and yourself and re-establish your wards.

CONCLUSION

The only thing you need to get started down the path of magic is yourself. Your power is hidden within, waiting to be tapped into. – Ambrosia Hawthorne

Your power is much more incredible than you probably think. If there is one thing I'd like you to take away from the book, it is this: Within you, you have all the capabilities to protect yourself from psychic or magickal attack. Deep inside, there is a witch within you. All you have to do to be one is make that choice and set yourself on the road less traveled.

This book has been a comprehensive guide for protection magick, covering proactive protection, shielding, hex-breaking, reversal magick, and banishing. Knowing about all of these various spell types before you start your journey will put you in good stead to go forward and cast magick. Setting up wards is excellent practice and will acclimatize you to magick so that you can then go on to other spell types, such as those for prosperity or finding love.

However, if you are already an accomplished witch, this book has been an addition to your pre-existing library of magickal tomes. It will have supplemented your knowledge of protection magick as well as given you prompts to delve deeper into your practice by considering your own ethical framework as well as ways to adapt spells for your own purposes and even design your own.

If this book has whetted your whistle, you may enjoy my other books on various magickal subjects. I would strongly advise that you never read just one book on magick and think the job is done. The path of the witch is full of spell casting, yes, but to be able to do that, you need to build your knowledge of the field.

I'll end with one final piece of advice: Go forth, delve deeper into magick, and practice, practice, practice. You will achieve things you never thought possible.

Remain magickal, my friends.

REFERENCES

Alejandrez-Prasad, J. (2023, May 22). *Latina Bruja's guide to an egg cleanse (Huevo Limpia).* Pop Sugar. https://www.popsugar.com/smart-living/how-to-do-egg-cleanse-huevo-limpia-ritual-48963277

Alexander, S. (2014). *The modern guide to witchcraft: Your complete guide to witches, covens, & spells.* Adams Media. Amazon Kindle store.

"Am I cursed?" 10 symptoms of magickal danger. (n.d.). Old World Witchcraft. https://oldworldwitchcraft.com/pages/am-i-cursed-10-symptoms-of-magickal-danger

Angel, G. (2013, January 7). *Fascinus & the winged phallus tattoo.* UCL. https://blogs.ucl.ac.uk/researchers-in-museums/2013/01/07/fascinus-the-winged-phallus-tattoo/

Aphrodite titles. (n.d). Theoi Project. https://www.theoi.com/Cult/AphroditeTitles.html

Auryn, M. (2020a). *Psychic witch: A metaphysical guide to meditation, magick & manifestation.* Llewellyn Publications.

Auryn, M. (2020b, January 4). *The difference between charms, amulets & talismans.* Modern Witch. https://www.patheos.com/blogs/modernwitch/2020/01/the-difference-between-charms-amulets-talismans/

Baker, J. (2014). *The cunning man's handbook: The practice of English folk magic 1550–1900.* Avalonia.

Benedetti, A. (2022, October 28). 40 empowering witch quotes that will make you feel wicked. *She Explores Life.* https://sheexploreslife.com/quotes-about-witches/

Beyer, C. (2019, June 5). The five element symbols of fire, water, air, earth, spirit. *Learn Religions.* https://www.learnreligions.com/elemental-symbols-4122788

Blakemore, E. (2016, August 22). A guide to ancient magic. *Smithsonian Magazine.* https://www.smithsonianmag.com/smart-news/guide-ancient-magic-180960129/

Burkert, W. (1987). *Greek religion: Archaic and classical* (J. Raffan, Trans.) Wiley-Blackwell. (Original work published 1977).

Brethauer, A. (2023, May 17). Egg cleanse meaning and powerful ritual interpretation. *The Peculiar Brunette.* https://www.thepeculiarbrunette.com/egg-cleanse-meaning-ritual-interpretation/

Chamberlain, L. (2017a, June 6). Magical properties of colors. *Wicca Living.* https://wiccaliving.com/magical-properties-colors/

Chamberlain, L. (2017b, June 16). Clearing and charging ritual tools and magical ingredients. *Wicca Living.* https://wiccaliving.com/clearing-charging-ritual-tools/

Clark, B. (n.d.). Agathos Daimon. *Hellenion.* https://www.hellenion.org/festivals/agathos-daimon/

Cunningham, S. (1989). *Wicca: A guide for the solitary practitioner.* Llewellyn Publications US

Cunningham, S. (2007). *Cunningham's encylopedia of magical herbs.* Llewellyn.

Cunningham, S. (2021). *Cunningham's encylopedia of crystal, gem & metal magic.* Llewellyn.

Curses, hexes, and jinxes: What's the difference? (2020, October 23). Tea and Rosemary. https://teaandrosemary.com/curses-hexes-and-jinxes-whats-the-difference/

Dieleman, J. (2015). The materiality of textual

amulets in Ancient Egypt. In: D. Boschung and J. N. Bremmer (Eds.), *The materiality of magic* (pp. 23–58). Wilhelm Fink.

Fowler, R. L. (1995). *Greek magic, Greek religion.* Illinois Classical Studies. https://www.jstor.org/stable/23065394

Golding, W. R. J. (2013). Perceptions of the serpent in the Ancient Near East: Its Bronze Age role in apotropaic magic, healing and protection (Identifier: http://hdl.handle.net/10500/13353) [Masters Dissertation, University of South Africa]. UNISA Institutional Repository.

Habib, R. R. (2017). *Protective magic in Ancient Greece: Patterns in the material culture of apotropaia from the archaic to Hellenistic Periods* (Publication number FSU_SUMMER2017_Habib_fsu_0071E_13857) [Doctoral Dissertation, Florida State University]. DigiNole.

Harding, J. (2016, June 6). *Sheela Na Gig.* Encylcopedia Britannica. https://www.britannica.com/art/Sheela-Na-Gig

Hargitai, Q. (2018, February 19). *The strange power of the 'evil eye'.* BBC Culture. https://www.bbc.com/culture/article/20180216 -the-strange-power-of-the-evil-eye

Hart, A. (2023, August 19). *Why ancestral curses are so hard to break and how to do it.* The Traveling Witch. https://thetravelingwitch.com/blog/why-generational-curses-are-so-hard-to-break-and-how-to-do-it

Horne, R. (2019). *Folk witchcraft: A guide to lore, land, and the familiar spirit for the solitary practitioner.* Moon over the Mountain Press.

Kelley, G. (2020). Doctor Beaky, the Four Thieves, and De Fabulis Pestis. Contemporary Legend. https://scholarworks.iu.edu/journals/index.php /cl/article/view/35143

Kharis (Χάρις); our relationship with the gods.

(2012, July 26). Baring the Aegis. http://baringtheaegis.blogspot.com/2012/07/kharis-our-relationship-with-gods.html

King, G. (2016). *The British book of spells & charms*. Troy Books.

Konstantinos. (2002). *Vampires: The occult truth*. Llewellyn. Amazon Kindle store.

Kraig, D. M. (2010). *Magic vs. magick*. Llewellyn. https://www.llewellyn.com/blog/2010/05/magic-vs-magick/

Gottlieb, K. (2017). *Cultural appropriation in contemporary neopaganism and witchcraft*. (Publication number 304) [Honours dissertation, The University of Maine]. Digital Commons@U Maine. https://digitalcommons.library.umaine.edu/cgi/viewcontent.cgi?article=1303&context=honors

Larson, E. (2019, April 11–13). *Transitional magic: Apotropaic wands as an allegory for the Middle Kingdom* [Conference presentation]. Proceedings of the National Conference On Undergraduate Research (NCUR), Kennesaw State University Kennesaw, Georgia.

Lóránt, V. (2016). Fascinum in Aquicum — protection against evil eye. Phallic amulets in a Roman City. In: H. Erzsébet (Eds.), *Budapest Régiségei* (pp. 63–76). Budapesti Történeti Múzeum.

Meier, A. C. (2019, May 13). *Is there a witch bottle in your house?* Jstor Daily. https://daily.jstor.org/is-there-a-witch-bottle-in-your-house/

Merriam-Webster. (n.d.-a). Occult. *Merriam-Webster*. https://www.merriam-webster.com/dictionary/occult

Merriam-Webster. (n.d.-b). Sigil. *Merriam-Webster*. https://www.merriam-webster.com/dictionary/sigil

Merriam-Webster. (n.d.-c). Ward. *Merriam-Webster*. https://www.merriam-webster.com/dictionary/ward

Montemayor, C. (2023, September 12). *What percentage of men cheat?*. Brides. https://www.brides.com/what-percentage-of-men-cheat-5114527

Moral Relativism. (2022). Ethics Unwrapped. https://ethicsunwrapped.utexas.edu/glossary/moral-relativism

Morningbird. (2023, June 12). *What is a taglock & how it's used in magick.* Magickal Spot. https://magickalspot.com/taglock/

Murphy, J. M. (1990). *Black religion and 'black magic': Prejudice and projection in images of African-derived religions.* Religion, 20(4), 323–339. https://doi.org/10.1016/0048-721X(90)90115-M

Murphy, K. and Susulla, C. (2016). *Secrets of ancient magic: The power of spells, curses, & omens.* Expedition Magazine. https://www.penn.museum/sites/expedition/secrets-of-ancient-magic/

Newman, C. L. (2023). "Savages and sable subjects": White fear, racism, and demonization of New Orleans voodoo in the nineteenth century. Madison Historcal Review, 20(6). https://commons.lib.jmu.edu/mhr/vol20/iss1/6

Offerings to gods and ancestors: Paganism basics. (2018, June 6). Otherworldly Oracle. https://otherworldlyoracle.com/basics-pagan-offerings-to-gods-ancestors/

Olivelle, P. (2023, May 18). Karma. *Encyclopedia Britannica.* https://www.britannica.com/topic/karma

1196 — dried cat. (2021). Museum of Magic and Witchcraft. https://museumofwitchcraftandmagic.co.uk/object/dried-cat/

Parlett, D. (1999). *Tarot.* Encylopedia Britannica. https://www.britannica.com/topic/tarot

Pennick, N. (2021). *The ancestral power of amulets, talismans and mascots: Folk magic in witchcraft & religion.* Destiny Books.

Pinch, G. (2011, February 17). *Ancient Egyptian magic.* BBC History. https://www.bbc.co.uk/history/ancient/egyptians/magic_01.shtml

Porter, G. (2021). *Prayers and protection magick to destroy witchcraft: Banish curses, negative energy & psychic attacks; break spells, evil soul ties & covenants; protect & release favors.* Amazon Kindle store.

Protection Quotes. (n.d.) Bookroo. https://bookroo.com/quotes/protection

Purification in Hellenismos. (2013, July 8). Baring the Aegis. http://baringtheaegis.blogspot.com/2013/07/purification-in-hellenismos.html

Raine, A. (2012). *The gray witch's grimoire.* John Hunt Publishing. Amazon Kindle store.

The Rider Waite Smith deck. (n.d.). Tarot Heritage. https://tarot-heritage.com/history-4/the-rider-waite-smith-deck/

Saint Thomas, S. (2018, September 25). *Color magic: A witch's guide to color meanings and energies.* Allure. https://www.allure.com/story/color-magic-witchcraft-meanings-guide

Saint Thomas, S. (2020, March 24). *Your guide to the zodiac signs and their elements: Fire, earth, air, and water.* Allure. https://www.learnreligions.com/four-classical-elements-2562825

Schwarcz, J. (2022, February 4). *The evil eye.* McGill Office for Science and Society. https://www.mcgill.ca/oss/article/pseudoscience/evil-eye

Sebastiani, A. (2018, July 4). *20 simple yet effective cleansing & purification techniques.* Lady Althaea. https://www.ladyalthaea.com/everyday-is-magickal/cleansing-purification-pt-4

Smith, E. W. (2022, July 11). *These 47 witch quotes are actually magic.* Cosmopolitan. https://www.cosmopolitan.com/lifestyle/a3530 2526/best-witch-quotes/

13 best witch quotes to get you into the October spirit. (2020). The Wholesome Witch. https://www.thewholesomewitch.com/best-witch-quotes/

Thorne, T. (2020). *Protection spells of a wicked witch.* Hentopan Publishing. Amazon Kindle store.

Top 30 quotes on self defense. (n.d.). Girls Who Fight. https://www.girlswhofight.co/post/top-30-quotes-on-self-defense

Uncrossing: Removing negative energy. (2021). Kate's Magik. https://www.katesmagik.com/blogs/news/uncr ossing

Versnel, H. S. (1991). *Beyond cursing: The appeal to justice in judicial prayers.* In C. A. Faraone and D. Obbink (Eds.), *Magika hiera: Ancient Greek magic & religion* (pp. 60–106). Oxford University Press.

Vink, F. (2016). *The principles of apotropaic magic on Middle Kingdom wands.* Ancient Egypt.

Virginia. (2019, February 1). *Ancient Greek votive offerings in antiquity: Gifts to the gods.* Ancient & Oriental. *Antiquities.* https://www.antiquities.co.uk/blog/divinity-religion/ancient-greek-votive-offerings-in-antiquity-gifts-to-the-gods/

Visconti, S. (2019). *The complete tarot: Learn the tarot for beginners & advanced (2-in-1 bundle).* Self-published. Amazon Kindle store.

Volandes, S. (2020, May 14). *The history of the evil eye, an ancient symbol of protection.* Town & Country. https://www.townandcountrymag.com/style/je

welry-and-watches/a32446159/evil-eye-jewelry-history/

Webster, R. (2004, April 19). *Amulets, talismans, & charms.* Llewellyn. https://www.llewellyn.com/journal/article/583

What is a psychic attack? (2022, November 11). College of Psychic Studies. https://www.collegeofpsychicstudies.co.uk/enlighten/what-is-a-psychic-attack/

What is magic? Aleister Crowley explains. (2020). Faena Aleph. https://www.faena.com/aleph/what-is-magic-aleister-crowley-explains

Wigington, P. (2017, March 17). *Evoke & invoke.* Learn Religions. https://www.learnreligions.com/evoke-and-invoke-2561892

Wigington, P. (2018a, January 5). *Color magic—magical color correspondences.* Learn Religions. https://www.learnreligions.com/color-magic-magical-correspondences-4105405

Wigington, P. (2018b, March 14). *How to cast a circle for a pagan ritual.* Learn Religions. https://www.learnreligions.com/how-to-cast-a-circle-2562859

Wigington, P. (2018c, December 23). *The Wiccan Rede.* Learn Religions. https://www.learnreligions.com/the-wiccan-rede-2562601

Wiginton, P. (2019a, March 31). *Pagan offerings to the gods.* Learn Religions. https://www.learnreligions.com/offerings-to-the-gods-2561949

Wigington, P. (2019b, May 6). *The four classical elements.* Learn Religions. https://www.learnreligions.com/four-classical-elements-2562825

Wigington, P. (2020, September 21). *9 things to keep on your ancestor altar.* Llewellyn.

https://www.llewellyn.com/journal/article/284
3

Wilson, D. R (2019, April 26). *Are essential oils safe? 13 things to know before use.* Health Line. https://www.healthline.com/health/are-essential-oils-safe

Witchcraft: Eight myths and misconceptions. (n.d.). English Heritage. https://www.english-heritage.org.uk/learn/histories/eight-witchcraft-myths/

Woodfield, K. (2022). *Sigil magick: 5 steps to create sigils to manifest your goals.* Self-published. Amazon Kindle store.

Subscribe To Sofia Visconti

As a subscriber you will receive a Free Gift + You wil be the first to hear about new books, articles and more exclusives just for you

CLICK HERE

www.ingramcontent.com/pod-product-compliance
Lightning Source LLC
Chambersburg PA
CBHW071424150726
48000CB00001B/464